the Flying Biscuit cafe

COOKBOOK

the Flying Biscuit cafe

COOKBOOK

DELIA CHAMPION

Gibbs Smith, Publisher
TO ENRICH AND INSPIRE HUMANKIND
Salt Lake City | Charleston | Santa Fe | Santa Barbara

First Edition
11 10 09 08 07 5 4 3 2 1

Text © 2007 Delia Champion

Published by
Gibbs Smith, Publisher
P.O. Box 667
Layton, Utah 84041

Orders: 1.800.835.4993
www.gibbs-smith.com

Designed by Black Eye Design
Printed and bound in the U.S.A

Library of Congress Cataloging-in-Publication Data

Champion, Delia.
 The Flying Biscuit Cafe cookbook / Delia Champion. — 1st ed.
    p. cm.
 Includes index.
 ISBN-13: 978-1-4236-0293-4
 ISBN-10: 1-4236-0293-5
 1. Cookery, American—Southern style. 2. Flying Biscuit Cafe.
I. Title.

 TX715.2.S68C48 2007
 641.5975—dc22
                        2007020605

This book is dedicated to my grandmother,
who always told me I could do anything.

Contents

Thank you to . . .

Every Biscuit employee . . . past and present . . . the heart and soul of the Biscuit. So many of these recipes come from the employees, who have influenced the way the Flying Biscuit cooks.

The customers, many who have become family . . . for gracing our doors and allowing us the privilege to serve you.

Emily Saliers... for helping turn a simple dream into reality.

Ebrima Ceesay... for being a constant force and a source of inspiration and for keeping the important things in life simple and clear.

To the people who really made this book happen... Lauren Mross and Rama Roy (creative inspiration), Mary "Sniff" Cromer (making sure it always smells good), Gina Henshen (the motivator), and especially Gerlinda Grimes and Stacy Braukman (the muses), who took oral histories and turned them into written words that make great stories.

My white-collar advisers, Mindy Planer, Robert Wagner, Robert Wilson, Debra Golymbieski, and especially Shelton Gorelick, who is ALWAYS right.

Elaine McLure... for giving a girl a chance.

Bunny Carlson… for her kind words, support, and spirit.

Mr. and Mrs. Lee… who helped the Biscuit grow from the first day.

John Amend… a driving force behind the Biscuit's new partnership (and for being such a great thinker).

Steve LaMastra and the Raving Brands family… for your commitment to the future of the Biscuit, and for being the greatest partners a small business could hope for.

My families in Florida and North Carolina.

John Ryan and Wesley Chenault… for being the best family one could ever choose! and always being available to taste test.

Everyone at Gibbs Smith, Publisher, who make the magic of a book happen, and Christopher Robbins and Melissa Barlow—an editor who should win an award for patience.

And a very special and most important thank you to Wendy Weiner… for creating the graphics that make the Biscuit fly, for keeping it fresh, and for oh! so much more.

Foreword: It Takes a Village to Make a Biscuit

Over a decade ago, Delia Champion was waiting tables at Indigo Coastal Grille, a wonderful seafood restaurant in Atlanta. I used to eat there fairly frequently, and I always asked for Delia because she was this burst of light and energy. Over time, we became friends. She used to talk about her dream of opening up a place where you could eat breakfast all day, with a bottomless cup of hot coffee, good wholesome food, and a fair price. It would be a place where the community, in all of its diversity, could gather to share meals, talk, celebrate life's milestones, read the paper, or just plain old hang out. Everybody in the restaurant business who worked and slept late needed a place to eat breakfast any time they wanted. Delia figured they weren't the only ones.

Before Delia knew, friends came around to chip in one way or another and start to make that simple dream a reality. Some of us loaned money, others painted and knew how to get paint cheaply, some went to the Memorial Drive flea market and picked out tables and chairs, Polly made pottery plates and cups, and many learned how to flip eggs for the first time. The tiny location in Candler Park, with its twenty-one seats, plug-in cash machine, and purple ceiling, was scrubbed spotless by a team of friends and workers, and the original Flying Biscuit Cafe opened its doors in 1993. Delia and the other owners, Missy and Cynthia, had no idea what they were in for! The lines stretched down the sidewalk and wrapped around the corner. When those plates of steaming, heavenly biscuits with a side of April Moon's Cranberry Apple Butter arrived, people just couldn't get enough. They came in droves, eating biscuits in the morning and biscuits at night.

I made the Flying Biscuit my destination for any occasion. Amy and I even had a record release party there. With friends and family, over plates of Love Cakes and bowls of hearty soup, I have celebrated weddings, adoptions, new jobs, and life changes. We've had therapy sessions and marked the passing of loved ones. We've watched the seasons change and return. Life takes place at the Biscuit with its bustling, friendly staff, diverse community, and good food. After all these years, with two locations and a bakery, the Flying Biscuit has spread her wings. But she started as a pinpoint of a dream with a team of people who came together and made it happen. The Flying Biscuit is everyone's neighborhood.

Now enjoy the heart and soul of this special place in these recipes. Bring the community to your table. Make a ruckus, laugh loud, and dream big. Anything is possible—but you know it takes a village.

Emily Saliers,
Indigo Girl and Biscuit Patron

Introduction: For the Love of Biscuits

The Flying Biscuit Cafe Cookbook is a compilation of favorites. From customers' favorite recipes to favorite moments seared in Flying Biscuit history, this inspirational cookbook will have an instant place in the kitchen.

Delia Champion grew up in the restaurant business. Her parents owned a New Jersey taproom, where locals would trade their fresh produce (New Jersey is the garden state after all!) for a hearty meal, an icy cold brew, and lots of entertaining conversation. The taproom was a fixture in the community, and Delia always enjoyed the energy and excitement of cooking for a crowd.

In 1993, Delia and friends opened the first Flying Biscuit Cafe in Candler Park, a funky neighborhood in southeast Atlanta. Opening to rave reviews, the Flying Biscuit was an immediate hit and was named one of Atlanta's top ten restaurants. The accolades and popularity mounted (*Bon Appetit* Favorite Places, *Gourmet* Top Places, Frommer's Travel Recommendation, Zagat Guide Excellence Award, *Elle* Magazine City Guide, *Rachael Ray's $40 a Day*, O! Pure Oxygen feature, and of course the Turner South Blue Ribbon Winner for Best Southern Breakfast). In 2000, the Midtown location opened, which was greeted by the same frenzy as the original.

Plans for the future include expansion and franchise opportunities while maintaining the culture, the food, and the feel of The Flying Biscuit Cafe, and making it relevant to a new generation of customers.

BISCUIT

LOVE

Delia Champion has always loved breakfast. And not just in the morning. She remembers fondly her family tradition of Sunday supper, where everyone would gather for a big afternoon meal every Sunday after church. At night, because they'd filled up on a tasty pot roast or a plump roasted chicken, Delia and her family would eat breakfast — for dinner. To her, "It was a thrill. I always loved that. It was such a treat. And I always knew that we would serve breakfast all day. Any time you want, at the Flying Biscuit, you'll have breakfast." For her, breakfast is not just delicious, it's hearty and healthy, and who wouldn't want to be able to enjoy it any time of day?

This reflects her entire approach to the Biscuit — not to try to guess what people might like in a restaurant, but to take what she knew she liked and share it with the world. Her vision was not always entirely practical, though. One of her early ideas involved toasters. "Every little table would have a toaster," she recalls with a grin, "a pretty little pastel toaster. The server would bring the bread to the table and the guest would get to toast their own toast, so when it popped up it would be especially hot and they could butter it themselves. And we would do some kind of fancy butters and jams on the table."

Thankfully, biscuits ended up trumping toast. They became the centerpiece — and namesake — of the restaurant. "I think bread is the basis of every meal — it really is the staff of life. I think all great restaurants have great bread. We just chose the biscuit." Biscuits are a southern staple; they symbolize a certain old-fashioned hospitality, warmth, and love. They also happen to be extraordinarily versatile. You can open your refrigerator or pantry, see what you've got, and mix almost anything into a biscuit. Savory, sweet, it's all good. It's also easy and fun.

Biscuits are a type of quick bread, which requires only a few simple ingredients—and the rest is up to your imagination and appetite. As Delia puts it, "When you think about it, you're taking a flat hockey puck and you're putting it in the oven, and it rises and becomes beautiful and edible and it's so good. It's magic! It's still magic. I never get tired of it."

As for the name, Delia's friend and Indigo Coastal Grille coworker "Mickey" Michelle thought it up during a rafting trip down the Colorado River. Each evening, sleeping out under the stars, she saw a sky more beautiful than the night before. One evening, it just hit her. She came back from her vacation, excited to tell Delia the news: "I have the name for your restaurant."

Delia replied, "Really, what?"

"The Flying Biscuit."

Delia loved it, but just before opening day, when it came time to settle once and for all on the name, she hesitated. She knew that the word biscuit might draw fewer customers at night. But she stayed true to her original idea, and she believed (and still believes) that success comes from doing one thing and doing it the best that you can. "I thought, you know what? Nothing else will do. I cannot even consider naming it something else. It has to be The Flying Biscuit."

Famous Flying Biscuits

This is how we begin each day! We only use White Lily, the true southern flour.

3 cups all-purpose flour

1 tablespoon double-acting baking powder

¾ teaspoon salt

4 tablespoons granulated sugar, divided

6 tablespoons unsalted butter, at room temperature

1 ½ cups light cream*

⅓ cup half-and-half

Preheat oven to 350 degrees F. Line a sheet pan with parchment paper.

Combine flour, baking powder, salt, and 3 tablespoons sugar in a large mixing bowl. Cut butter into ½ tablespoon-sized bits and add to the flour. Using your hands, work the butter into the dry ingredients—don't hold back. I suggest closing your eyes, turning the music up, and enjoying the texture of flour mixing with butter. Mix until butter is cut to the size of small peas.

Make a well in the center of the flour and then pour in the light cream. Stir the dry ingredients into the wet by using your hand in a circular fashion, knocking the flour mix into the liquid. Stir just until dough comes together into a sticky ball. Turn dough onto a lightly floured surface and knead three times. Do not overwork the dough. Using a lightly floured rolling pin, roll the dough to a thickness of 1 inch. The correct thickness is the key to making your biscuits fly.

Dip a 2½-inch-diameter biscuit cutter in flour, then cut the dough. Repeat until all the dough has been cut. Do not twist the cutter—apply pressure straight down then pull back evenly. Scraps can be massed together and re-rolled one time.

Place the biscuits on the prepared sheet pan, leaving about ¼ inch between them. Brush the tops of the biscuits with the half-and-half (about 1 tablespoon per biscuit) and sprinkle with remaining sugar. Bake for 20 to 23 minutes. Biscuits will be golden brown on top and flaky in the center when done.

MAKES 8 TO 12 BISCUITS, DEPENDING ON THE SIZE OF THE CUTTER

*If your local store does not have light cream, you can substitute 1 cup half-and-half.

Adapted from a recipe by April Moon.

Sweet Potato Biscuits

These fly off the plate!

3 cups all-purpose flour

1 tablespoon baking powder

½ teaspoon double-acting baking soda

¾ teaspoon salt

3 tablespoons packed light brown sugar

Generous pinch ground ginger

1 tablespoon freshly grated orange zest

6 tablespoons unsalted butter, chilled and cut
    into small pieces

1 cup mashed cooked sweet potato

⅔ cup buttermilk

6 tablespoons unsalted butter, melted

Preheat oven to 370 degrees F. Line a sheet pan with parchment paper.

In a mixing bowl, combine flour, baking powder, baking soda, salt, brown sugar, ginger, and orange zest. Using your hands, work the butter into the dry ingredients until the pieces of butter are the size of small peas. Mash, stir, mix it in, smoosh, squish, have at it, get down on it, do it to it, soup it up, and get it good 'n' ready before you add those sweet potatoes! Now add in the sweet potatoes. Use your hands, dig in, and don't hold back.

Add buttermilk and mix with your hands just until the dough comes together and still sticks to your fingers. Once you add the buttermilk, it is critical that you do not over mix.

Turn dough onto a lightly floured surface and knead four to six times. Using lightly floured hands, pat out the dough to a thickness of 1 inch. Dip a 2½-inch-diameter biscuit cutter in flour, then cut the dough. Repeat until all the dough has been cut. Do not twist the cutter — apply pressure straight down then pull back evenly. Scraps can be gathered together and re-rolled one time. Using a fork, prick the tops of each biscuit 3 times.

Place the biscuits on the prepared sheet pan, leaving about ¼ inch between them. Brush the tops of each biscuit with the melted butter (about ½ tablespoon per biscuit). Bake for 20 to 25 minutes. Biscuits will be golden brown on the top and flaky in the center when done.

MAKES 8 TO 12 BISCUITS, DEPENDING ON THE SIZE OF THE CUTTER

Super Easy Cheesy Biscuits

This fun recipe is a great way to introduce kids to baking!

2 cups White Lily Biscuit Mix or your favorite dry
   biscuit mix

⅔ cup whole milk

½ cup grated cheddar cheese

¼ cup grated Parmigiano-Reggiano cheese

4 tablespoons unsalted butter

½ teaspoon finely minced fresh garlic

Preheat oven to 450 degrees F.

Combine biscuit mix, milk, and cheese in a large mixing bowl. Get the kids to give it a great big stir. Drop by tablespoon onto an ungreased baking sheet. Bake for 10 to 12 minutes, or until bottoms are lightly browned.

Melt butter and stir in chopped garlic. Brush over warm biscuits.

MAKES 8 TO 12 BISCUITS

THE ACCOLADES: BISCUIT LOVE

With a name like "The Flying Biscuit," it's inevitable that the media focuses on the subject of biscuits. Through the years, Delia's response to the question "What makes your biscuits so special?" has never changed: "Our biscuits are made with butter, light cream, and a lot of love."

Delia's philosophy has always been to make every decision from a place of love, and it will filter down from the employees to the customers through the food. In fact, it's always been about so much more than just the food... It's about the experience as a whole at the Biscuit.

What a great recipe for success: lots of hard work, spectacular employees, and that special ingredient — love! That's what keeps the old customers coming back and the new customers discovering this special place.

Cheddar and Jalapeño Biscuits

Here's a biscuit that bites and that's good!

1 ½ cups all-purpose flour

2 teaspoons double-acting baking powder

½ teaspoon baking soda

½ teaspoon salt

2 tablespoons cold unsalted butter, cut into bits

1 cup grated sharp cheddar cheese

¼ cup diced pickled jalapeño peppers
    (wear rubber gloves when handling peppers)

1 cup sour cream

Place rack in middle of oven. Preheat oven to 425 degrees F. Line a baking sheet with parchment paper; set aside.

In a medium bowl, sift together flour, baking powder, baking soda, and salt. Add butter, and blend the mixture until it resembles coarse meal. Stir in cheese and jalapeños, add sour cream, and stir the mixture until it just forms a soft but not sticky dough. Knead the dough gently six times on a lightly floured surface, and then roll or pat out to ½-inch thickness. With a 3 ½-inch cookie cutter, cut out 6 rounds. Bake rounds on baking sheet for 15 to 17 minutes, or until golden brown.

MAKES 8 TO 12 BISCUITS

Organic Oatmeal Biscuits

This style of biscuit is a cross between a scone and a cookie.

2 cups organic rolled oats

2 cups whole wheat flour

1 cup unsalted butter, chilled
   and cut into pieces

⅓ cup packed dark brown sugar

1 ¾ teaspoons double-acting baking powder

1 ½ teaspoons salt

½ cup whole milk

In a food processor, coarsely chop oats and transfer to a large bowl.

Pulse flour, butter, brown sugar, baking powder, and salt in food processor until mixture becomes a coarse meal. Add milk and blend until mixture just forms a sticky dough. Add oat mixture and knead three to four times until just barely mixed. Do not over mix.

Turn dough out onto a lightly floured surface. Halve dough and pat each half into a 6 x 3-inch rectangle. Wrap rectangles separately in plastic wrap. Refrigerate until firm (2 to 12 hours).

Preheat oven to 375 degrees F. Cut loaves into 24 (½-inch-thick) slices. Bake on a large ungreased sheet pan on middle rack of oven for about 20 minutes.

MAKES 24 BISCUITS

Itty Bitty Biscuit Buns

Will keep you in that teeny weeny biscuit bikini.

For Biscuit Buns

2 ½ cups all-purpose flour

1 teaspoon salt

1 tablespoon double-acting baking powder

½ teaspoon baking soda

⅓ cup unsalted butter, at room temperature

1 cup buttermilk

For Filling

¼ cup unsalted butter, at room temperature

1 cup plus 2 tablespoons orange marmalade

¼ cup packed light brown sugar

For Orange Drizzle Icing

2 ½ cups confectioners' sugar

¼ cup freshly squeezed orange juice

1 teaspoon butter, at room temperature

2 tablespoons cream cheese, at room temperature

¼ teaspoon pure vanilla extract

2 tablespoons finely grated orange zest

To make Biscuit Buns

Combine flour, salt, baking powder, and baking soda in a large bowl. Cut butter into ½ tablespoon-sized bits and add to the flour mixture. Mix until butter is the size of small peas.

Add buttermilk and mix until well combined. Roll out dough on a lightly floured surface until about a thickness of ¾ inch. Cut into 10 to 12 rounds with a small round biscuit cutter. Roll out each individual biscuit until it is 5 inches in diameter and ¼ inch in thickness.

To fill Biscuit Buns

Preheat oven to 425 degrees F.

On each biscuit, layer 1 teaspoon butter, 1 ½ tablespoons marmalade, and 1 tablespoon brown sugar. Roll up each biscuit like a jelly roll and slice crosswise into 3 pinwheels of equal length. Place rolls in two ungreased 7 x 7-inch baking pans. Be sure the sides of the buns kiss. Bake for 10 to 12 minutes, or until golden brown. Let cool in pans on wire rack for 10 minutes while you prepare the icing… if you can!

To make Icing

Whisk together confectioners' sugar, orange juice, butter, cream cheese, vanilla, and orange zest until creamy and smooth. Drizzle over warm rolls.

MAKES 10 TO 12 SERVINGS

Pumpkin and Pecan Biscuits

A family tradition on the first cool fall morning of each year.

2 ¼ cups all-purpose flour

4 teaspoons double-acting baking powder

1 teaspoon ground ginger

1 teaspoon ground cinnamon

¾ teaspoon salt

½ teaspoon ground cardamom

½ cup chilled unsalted butter, cut into ½-inch pieces

½ cup packed canned pumpkin

¼ cup plus 2 tablespoons chilled whipping cream, divided

⅓ cup packed light brown sugar

4 tablespoons honey, divided

½ cup chopped pecans, toasted

Preheat oven to 375 degrees F. Line a large sheet pan with parchment paper.

In a large bowl, mix together flour, baking powder, ginger, cinnamon, salt, and cardamom. Add butter and, using hands, mix until mixture resembles coarse meal.

In a medium bowl whisk together pumpkin, ¼ cup cream, brown sugar, and 2 tablespoons honey.

Add pumpkin mixture and chopped pecans to dry ingredients and stir until incorporated. Dough will be moist. Do not overwork.

Turn dough onto a lightly floured surface and knead four times. Roll out dough to a thickness of ¾ inch. Using a floured 2 ½-inch-diameter biscuit cutter, cut out 12 to 16 rounds. Scraps can be re-rolled one more time. Place biscuits on prepared sheet pan.

Mix remaining cream and honey in a small bowl. Brush biscuit mixture onto biscuit tops. Bake biscuits about 25 minutes, or until light golden, and cake tester or toothpick inserted into center comes out clean.

MAKES 12 TO 16 BISCUITS

Tip: To reheat, place foil-wrapped biscuits in a preheated 350-degree F oven for 7 to 10 minutes.

Orange Blossom Biscuits Topped with Peaches

A perfect top for a perfect bottom.

For Sprinkle

¼ cup granulated sugar

1 ½ teaspoons grated orange zest

For Biscuits

1 ½ cups all-purpose flour

½ cup yellow cornmeal

1 tablespoon baking powder

½ teaspoon salt

3 tablespoons brown sugar

½ cup unsalted butter, cut into ¼-inch pieces

⅔ cup whole milk

For Filling

2 pounds peaches, peeled, pitted, and cut into
    ½-inch-thick slices

⅓ cup granulated sugar

½ teaspoon pure vanilla extract

1 cup whipping cream

3 tablespoons confectioners' sugar

Fresh mint leaves (optional)

To make Sprinkle

In a small bowl, thoroughly mix sugar and orange zest, muddling with the back of a wooden spoon until mixture is pale orange goodness; set aside.

To make Biscuits

Preheat oven to 400 degrees F. Line a large sheet pan with parchment paper.

Mix flour, cornmeal, baking powder, salt, and brown sugar in a large bowl. Add butter, mixing with fingertips until mixture forms a coarse meal. Add milk and mix until dough is evenly moistened, adding more milk by tablespoonfuls if mixture is dry and does not hold together. Drop dough by heaping tablespoons onto prepared sheet pan, forming 8 to 10 mounds and spacing 1 ½ inches apart. Using lightly floured fingertips, pat each biscuit into a 2-inch round. Sprinkle the reserved orange sugar sprinkle over top. Bake biscuits about 18 minutes. Cool sheet pan on a wire rack.

To make Filling

In a large bowl, toss peaches, sugar, and vanilla; set aside to macerate, approximately 15 minutes, tossing occasionally.

Using electric mixer on high speed, whip cream and sugar in medium bowl until stiff peaks form.

Split the biscuits in half. Divide bottom halves among eight plates. Layer with ¼ cup macerated peaches and a dollop of whipped cream. Cover each with a biscuit top and garnish with mint if desired.

MAKES 8 TO 10 SERVINGS

HOW MANY BISCUITS SHOULD A BISCUIT-MAKER BAKE?

The night before opening day, the Biscuit-eers gathered around a table in their freshly painted dining room to plan their first batch of biscuits. Delia asked, "How many biscuits should we make tomorrow morning?"

Chef April Moon figured she had ten friends who would stop by. Missy Speert and Cynthia Moore, original co-owners of the Biscuit, thought they could round up fifteen guests each. Emily Saliers, the original investor, would certainly show up with a few friends. Finally, Delia reckoned she had a dozen or so former co-workers, from her server days, who might show up — if they weren't too tired.

"And," Delia said, "We should make a few extra. A total of ninety should be plenty... We don't want to have too many left over."

The next morning at 7:00, the Flying Biscuit served its inaugural breakfast. Guests got their first taste of those now-famous, enormous, sugar-sprinkled "flying" biscuits. That first batch of biscuits sold out by 11:00, and the Flying Biscuit had to close its doors for the day. Delia and the gang were left wondering if 120 biscuits might be enough for day two. As the story goes, they were wrong again.

BREAKFAST

ALL-STARS

Delia was the server who loved being a server. She spent countless evenings polishing silverware late into the night and having dreamy discussions with her co-workers: "If I owned this place… ," "If I won the lottery… " "If I could change the world… " Servers are nocturnal creatures. They get up late, they work late, and they sleep late. Delia usually began her day after 2:00 in the afternoon, more times than not with a craving for grits and eggs. But no restaurants served a decent breakfast in the late afternoon. So, Delia's dream was always the same: "If I owned a restaurant, I'd serve breakfast all day long."

"It's not that I thought I would open a restaurant," she says. "But it made me happy to imagine myself with a cozy little cafe filled with friends." The more Delia dreamed of herself as a restaurant owner, the bigger the idea became.

She actually went so far as to look into some possible locations. Back then, Sylvia's Atomic Cafe operated out of a funky little storefront, where the Flying Biscuit Cafe would eventually find its home. Delia talked to Sylvia a couple of times about taking over the space, but the idea seemed completely out of reach. Then, in the wee hours of the morning, as Delia was channel surfing before calling it a night, she stumbled onto what looked like a televangelist beseeching his flock, "Imagine what it would be like to live your life without fear." Once Delia realized it was not the Old Time Gospel Hour, but an infomercial selling the idea of living a life free from fear, she was hooked.

At first she was skeptical. "No way," Delia thought. "Fear is what keeps people alive." But she couldn't turn it off. The man on TV continued: "Imagine making decisions from a place of

no fear. Don't be afraid that people will tell you no. Don't be afraid that you might fail. Can you try it for thirty days? Just thirty days without fear?" She figured there must be a reason she was riveted, at 3:00 in the morning, to this infomercial. And she decided at that moment, maybe, for just one week, to live each day fearing absolutely nothing.

The next afternoon, driving past the Atomic Cafe, Delia was shocked to see Sylvia on the sidewalk, smashing an old upright piano to pieces. She wanted to pull over and see why Sylvia was so upset, but she thought, "Sylvia won't give me the time of day." Then she stopped and asked herself: remember the vow to live without fear for seven days? She was only one day in. So Delia forced herself to turn the car around and ask Sylvia why she was destroying her beloved piano on the sidewalk of McLendon Avenue. Sylvia told her that a large water main had broken on the block, and it was the last straw. As far as Sylvia was concerned, this was a sign to close the Atomic Cafe.

Fortunately, Delia took it as a sign as well—to contact the landlord and convince her that a server with a dream (and some financial backing from close friends) was capable of beating the odds and running a successful restaurant. After a few months, untold gallons of donated yellow and purple paint, and a group of friends working late into many a night, the Flying Biscuit Cafe opened its doors. The rest is history.

Sausage and Gravy

Featuring the Flying Biscuit's signature free-range chicken sausage. See box at bottom.

1 pound Flying Biscuit Signature Free Range Chicken Sausage or bulk breakfast sausage

½ cup unsalted butter

1 large diced white onion

1 teaspoon dried rosemary or 2 teaspoons chopped fresh rosemary

2 cloves garlic, chopped

1 teaspoon dried or 2 teaspoons chopped fresh thyme

3 teaspoons ground black pepper

2 tablespoons chopped parsley

¼ cup all-purpose flour

2 cups heavy cream

2 cups whole milk

Cayenne pepper

Salt

8 Flying Biscuits (see page 18) or any other bread to ladle gravy over

Brown sausage in a large, heavy saucepan over medium heat, breaking it with a spoon into medium-sized pieces. When the meat is thoroughly brown, drain the fat by putting the meat in a large colander; set aside.

Return the saucepan to medium heat, and melt the butter in it. Add onion, rosemary, garlic, thyme, black pepper, and parsley, and saute until the onions are translucent.

Add flour to the onions and stir until mixed completely. Add the drained sausage to the saucepan and stir to combine thoroughly. Add heavy cream and milk. Stir and simmer over low heat. Cook to desired thickness. If gravy becomes too thick, add small amounts of 2 percent milk. Add cayenne pepper and salt to taste.

Split biscuits in half and divide among eight plates. Ladle a heaping helping of gravy right on top.

SERVES 8

In addition to the biscuits, it's the sausage that sets the Flying Biscuit Cafe apart from other restaurants. We get our signature chicken sausage from Atlantan Michael Sabir, who puts his heart and soul — not to mention the finest, freshest ingredients — into this amazing sausage.

Biscuit French Toast

Works best with biscuits at least a day old.

6 Flying Biscuits (see page 18)

¼ cup granulated sugar

⅛ teaspoon salt

1 cup whole milk

1 ½ teaspoons pure vanilla extract

3 large eggs

Canola oil for griddle

Butter, at room temperature

Maple syrup, warmed

Using a serrated bread knife, slice the biscuits vertically from the top to bottom. Make two cuts per biscuit to yield 3 slices.

In a large bowl, combine sugar, salt, milk, vanilla, and eggs. Whisk all ingredients together until batter is light and frothy.

Lightly coat a large griddle or saute pan with canola oil and place over medium heat. Dip biscuit slices in batter, then place them on the preheated griddle. (The surface is properly heated when a few drops of cold water flicked onto it jump and sputter; if water just sits and slowly boils, the surface is not hot enough, and if it steams away immediately, it is too hot.) Cook until biscuit halves are light brown on both sides, about 3 to 5 minutes per side. Remove to a platter or individual plates, or keep warm in oven. Serve with butter and warm maple syrup. Works well with any stale bread.

SERVES 6

Banana Bread French Toast with Maple Cream Cheese

If your bananas are ready and you're not, just freeze them!

For Banana Bread

1 ½ cups mashed ripe bananas

¾ cup granulated sugar

⅔ cup nonfat vanilla yogurt

4 ½ tablespoons butter, melted and cooled

½ teaspoon pure vanilla extract

2 large eggs

2 ⅔ cups all-purpose flour

¾ teaspoon double-acting baking powder

1 teaspoon baking soda

¼ teaspoon salt

For Maple Cream Cheese

1 (8-ounce) package cream cheese, softened

1 cup butter at room temperature

1 cup confectioners' sugar

1 teaspoon pure vanilla extract

2 tablespoons pure maple syrup

For French Toast

¼ cup granulated sugar

⅛ teaspoon salt

1 ½ teaspoons pure vanilla extract

1 cup whole milk

3 large eggs

Canola oil

To make Banana Bread

Preheat oven to 350 degrees F. Lightly grease and flour two (1 ½-quart) loaf pans.

Combine bananas, sugar, yogurt, butter, vanilla, and eggs in a large bowl; whisk until smooth.

Sift together flour, baking powder, baking soda, and salt in a medium bowl. Add dry ingredients to wet ingredients, and fold just until combined. Do not over mix.

Divide batter evenly between the loaf pans. Bake for 30 to 35 minutes, or until a toothpick or cake tester inserted into the center of each loaf comes out clean. Remove loaves to a wire rack to cool completely, even overnight.

To make Maple Cream Cheese

Combine cream cheese, butter, confectioners' sugar, vanilla, and maple syrup in a medium bowl. Using an electric mixer on medium speed, beat until light and fluffy.

To make French Toast

Using a serrated knife, cut banana bread into 1-inch-thick slices.

In a large bowl, combine sugar, salt, vanilla, milk, and eggs. Whisk together all ingredients together until light and frothy.

Lightly coat a griddle or large saute pan with canola oil and place over medium heat. Dip banana bread slices into the batter, then place them on the preheated griddle. Cook until banana bread is light brown on both sides, about 3 minutes per side. Spread each slice with Maple Cream Cheese and serve.

SERVES 6 TO 8

Sweet Potato Pancakes

If you don't have leftover sweet potatoes, canned will do.

2 cups all-purpose flour

2 tablespoons granulated sugar

2 teaspoons double-acting baking powder

½ teaspoon salt

1 teaspoon ground cinnamon

¼ teaspoon ground nutmeg

1 cup milk

1 cup cooked, peeled, and mashed sweet potato

2 large eggs

½ cup unsalted butter, melted and cooled

½ teaspoon pure vanilla extract

Canola oil

In a large bowl, sift together flour, sugar, baking powder, salt, cinnamon, and nutmeg. In a second large bowl, whisk together milk, sweet potato, eggs, butter, and vanilla. Add dry ingredients into the wet ingredients and mix until batter is just blended. Do not over mix.

Preheat oven to 200 degrees F. Lightly coat a griddle or large saute pan with canola oil and preheat over medium heat. (The surface is properly heated when a few drops of cold water flicked onto it jump and sputter; if the water just sits and slowly boils, the surface is not hot enough, and if it steams away immediately, it is too hot.) Ladle ¼ cup batter per pancake. When bubbles appear, flip pancakes and cook until golden brown, about 3 to 5 minutes per side. Keep cooked pancakes warmed on an ovenproof plate, loosely covered with foil, in a preheated oven while you make the whole batch.

MAKES ABOUT 18 TO 22 PANCAKES AND SERVES 6 TO 8

Gingersnap Pancakes with Pecan Butter

You'll say, "Two snaps up and a pat!"

For Pecan Butter

¼ cup honey

1 cup unsalted butter, softened

½ cup chopped pecans, toasted

For Gingersnap Pancakes

Vegetable oil

2 cups whole wheat flour

1 ½ teaspoons baking soda

1 ½ teaspoons ground ginger

1 ½ teaspoons ground cinnamon

½ teaspoon salt

¼ teaspoon ground cloves

1 (12-ounce) can frozen apple juice concentrate, thawed

½ cup water

¼ cup unsalted butter, melted and cooled

2 large eggs

Maple syrup

To make Pecan Butter

In a medium bowl, using an electric mixer on low speed, slowly beat honey into butter. Add pecans and beat again. Serve at room temperature.

To make Gingersnap Pancakes

Lightly coat a griddle or large saute pan with vegetable oil and heat over medium heat.

In a large bowl, blend flour, baking soda, ginger, cinnamon, salt, and cloves. In a medium bowl, whisk apple juice concentrate, water, butter, and eggs. Add dry ingredients into the wet ingredients and mix until batter is just blended. Do not over mix.

For each pancake, ladle ¼ cup batter onto preheated griddle or saute pan. Cook pancakes until golden brown, about 3 minutes per side (they are ready to flip when little bubbles pop to the top of the uncooked side). Serve with Pecan Butter and maple syrup.

MAKES ABOUT 18 TO 22 PANCAKES AND SERVES 6

Simple Frittata

You say frittater... I say frittata!

½ cup fine virgin olive oil

4 cloves garlic, crushed

10 large eggs

½ cup freshly grated Parmesan cheese

⅓ cup grated fresh mozzarella cheese

⅓ cup sun-dried tomatoes, drained

⅓ cup heavy cream

¼ cup chopped scallions

1 teaspoon finely chopped fresh tarragon

1 teaspoon salt

¼ teaspoon freshly ground black pepper

Preheat the oven to 350 degrees F. Line a large sheet pan with parchment paper; set aside.

In a 12-inch ovenproof saute pan over very low heat, heat the oil. Saute the garlic in the oil until soft, about 10 minutes.

In a large bowl, vigorously beat eggs. Add olive oil and garlic, Parmesan, mozzarella, sun-dried tomatoes, cream, scallions, and tarragon. Add salt and pepper.

Spray saute pan with nonstick spray. Add egg mixture and cook over medium heat without stirring for 2 minutes or until the bottom begins to set. (Have patience and faith... your eggs will be fine if you just let them cook without disturbing the pan. Don't scramble!) Using a wide spatula, gently lift the edge of the frittata and tilt the pan so the uncooked egg seeps under. Continue this process until the bottom of the frittata is firm.

Place saute pan in oven and bake for 5 minutes. Eggs will rise and set across the top. Slide frittata onto a plate and cut into 6 wedges.

SERVES 6

Strata with Asparagus and Chicken Sausage

A strata is like a frittata… but notta.

1 teaspoon plus additional kosher salt

½ pound asparagus, trimmed and cut into 1-inch pieces

6 (¼-inch-thick) slices day-old bread, crusts removed

2 tablespoons extra virgin olive oil

6 ounces chicken sausage

10 large eggs

3 cups whole milk

Salt and freshly ground black pepper

2 cups grated fontina cheese, divided

In a medium stockpot over high heat, boil 6 cups of water. Add 1 teaspoon salt and asparagus. Cook asparagus until barely tender, about 5 minutes. Drain in a colander and spread onto a tea towel to dry.

Butter the bottom of a 13 x 9 x 2-inch baking dish. Line bottom of dish with bread.

In a large saute pan over medium heat, warm olive oil. Add sausage and brown thoroughly. Drain sausage in a colander and then put on top of bread in baking dish. Layer asparagus over sausage.

In a large bowl, whisk together eggs and milk. Add salt and pepper to taste. Stir in 1 ½ cups fontina cheese. Pour mixture over bread, sausage, and asparagus.

Cover baking dish with plastic wrap and refrigerate at least 4 hours or up to 24 hours.

Position rack in middle of oven. Preheat the oven to 350 degrees F. Top strata with remaining fontina cheese. Bake until golden and cooked through, about 30 to 45 minutes. Remove from oven and let stand for 15 minutes before serving.

SERVES 6

frittata *frit•ta•ta n.* An Italian dish made with fried beaten eggs, resembling a Spanish omelet.

strata *stra•ta n.* Oven-baked Italian custard mixed with stale bread.

Gratin of Eggs and Potatoes

A great use for leftover taters.

4 tablespoons unsalted butter, melted

2 cups panko bread crumbs

2 pounds russet potatoes (about 6 medium),
    peeled, cooked, and mashed (about 6 cups)

¼ cup crumbled blue cheese (or Gorgonzola)

12 large eggs

1 cup heavy cream

Salt and freshly ground black pepper

Preheat oven to 350 degrees F.

In a large saute pan, over medium-high heat, melt butter, then add bread crumbs. Toss to combine; set aside.

In a large bowl, mix potatoes with cheese. Spread mixture evenly in the bottom of a 9 x 13-inch glass baking dish. Make 12 small indentations or wells in the potato mixture.

Gently crack an egg into a wide, shallow bowl or cup and then gently slide the egg into one of the wells. Repeat one at a time with the remaining eggs until all the wells are filled. Gently pour cream over eggs and potatoes. Salt and pepper to taste. Scatter the top with the bread crumbs. Bake for 20 minutes, or until egg whites are firm and bread crumbs are browned. Scoop out potato and egg with a spoon and serve with crisp bacon. Best served in a shallow bowl.

SERVES 6

Biscuit-Style Eggs Benedict with Smoked Salmon

A new tradition for an old classic.

For Easy Hollandaise Sauce

3 tablespoons minced shallots

2 teaspoons dry mustard

1 ½ cups dry white wine

¾ cup whipping cream

Salt and pepper

3 large egg yolks

3 tablespoons chopped fresh dill

For Eggs Benedict

6 large, fluffy Flying Biscuits, sliced in half horizontally (see page 18)

8 ounces thinly sliced Nova Scotia smoked salmon (not lox)

3 tablespoons white wine vinegar

12 large eggs

To make Easy Hollandaise Sauce

Combine shallots and mustard in a medium saucepan. Gradually whisk in wine. Boil over high heat until mixture reduces to ½ cup, whisking often, about 10 minutes. Whisk in cream and season with salt and pepper. Whisk egg yolks into sauce. Whisk constantly until sauce thickens and an instant-read thermometer inserted into sauce registers 160 degrees F, about 4 minutes. Remove from heat. Add dill and whisk 1 minute.

To make Eggs Benedict

Toast cut side of biscuits under the broiler, until golden brown. Place 2 biscuit halves on each of six plates and top with smoked salmon.

Bring a large skillet of water to a boil; add vinegar. Reduce heat to a low simmer. Gently crack 2 eggs into a wide, shallow bowl or cup and gently slide the eggs into the simmering water. Poach until whites are set, but yolks are still runny, about 2 to 3 minutes. With a large slotted spoon, gently drain eggs and hold against a clean, dry kitchen towel to absorb as much water as possible. Transfer eggs onto biscuit halves. Repeat with remaining eggs, cooking two at a time. Spoon Easy Hollandaise Sauce on top of each poached egg and serve.

SERVES 6

Soft-Poached Eggs and Asparagus

Try it for dinner.

1 tablespoon fine virgin olive oil

1 tablespoon unsalted butter

1 clove garlic, thinly sliced

4 cups low-sodium vegetable stock

30 thin to medium asparagus spears, trimmed

12 button or cremini mushrooms, stems trimmed
and thinly sliced

12 large eggs

2 scallions, thinly sliced

Salt and freshly ground pepper

In a deep 12-inch diameter pan, over medium heat, heat oil and butter. Add garlic and cook until soft, about 3 minutes. Add stock and bring to a boil. Drop asparagus into stock and look for bright green color. The cooking time depends on thickness of the asparagus. Add mushrooms and reduce heat to low. Simmer for 3 minutes until asparagus is tender. Using tongs, place asparagus in bottoms of six shallow warmed soup bowls.

Crack 2 eggs into a bowl or cup and slide the eggs into simmering stock. Poach until whites are set but yolks are still runny, about 2 to 3 minutes. With a slotted spoon, transfer eggs into a bowl and ladle mushrooms and broth over the eggs. Poach eggs in batches until all are finished. Garnish with scallions and salt and pepper to taste. Repeat with the remaining eggs, cooking two at a time. Wonderful served with warm crusty bread to absorb the yolk and broth.

SERVES 6

Dr. Sylvan's Matzo Brei

Don't pass over this Passover treat!

10 large eggs

1 cup whole milk

Salt and freshly ground black pepper

10 sheets plain matzo

3 tablespoons unsalted butter

Pure maple syrup, warmed

8 tablespoons unsalted butter, at room
temperature and whipped

In a large bowl, whisk together eggs and milk; add salt and pepper to taste.

One at a time, hold the matzos under running water to quickly wet them on both sides without making them soggy. Drain in a colander. Break into 1-inch pieces and drop into egg wash. Stir to coat and soak for 10 minutes.

In a large nonstick skillet on medium heat, melt the butter. Add matzo and egg wash and let the mixture start to become firm and light brown. Toss and scramble until the eggs set. Serve with maple syrup and whipped butter.

SERVES 6

Banana, Chocolate Chip, and Pecan Scones

The most popular scone du jour!

4 cups all-purpose flour

1 ½ teaspoons double-acting baking powder

¾ cup plus 2 tablespoons granulated sugar

¼ teaspoon salt

3 medium ripe bananas

1 teaspoon pure vanilla extract

2 cups heavy cream, divided

2 cups semisweet chocolate chips

1 cup toasted pecan pieces

Position rack in middle of oven. Preheat oven to 350 degrees F. Line a sheet pan with parchment paper.

In a large mixing bowl, sift together flour, baking powder, ¾ cup sugar, and salt. In a small bowl, mash together bananas and vanilla.

Stir 1 ¾ cups cream into banana and vanilla mixture; add to flour mixture in the large bowl and stir. Do not over mix. Gently fold in chocolate chips and pecans just to combine. Do not overwork dough as the scones will become dense.

Turn dough out onto a lightly floured surface and knead gently two turns. Roll dough into a large circle 1 inch thick. Cut into 8 triangles.

Arrange on prepared sheet pan leaving 1 inch between scones. Brush top of scones with remaining cream and sprinkle with remaining sugar. Bake for 20 minutes. Scones will be golden on top and flaky in the middle when done.

SERVES 8

Peach Butter

Great slathered on biscuits, pancakes, and French toast. A Flying Biscuit favorite is a BLP sandwich: crisp turkey bacon, Bibb lettuce, and peach butter on a toasted day-old biscuit.

2 large ripe peaches, peeled, pitted, and finely
    chopped
½ cup unsalted butter, at room temperature
1 tablespoon honey

In a medium bowl, combine all ingredients and stir until combined. Store refrigerated in an air-tight container. Best served at room temperature.

MAKES 1 CUP

Omelets in a Bag

Great for kids. Prep your veggies the night before, and let everyone create their own masterpiece!

2 large eggs
1 quart ziplock freezer bag
1 tablespoon grated cheese, any kind

1 tablespoon of any other ingredient you like in your omelet (such as bacon, onion, tomato, basil, etc.)

Crack eggs right into the freezer ziplock bag. Add cheese and other optional ingredients. Seal the bag. Squish the bag to mix ingredients. "Burp" the air out of the bag and then drop baggie into boiling water. Boil for exactly 13 minutes. Carefully remove baggie, with tongs, from water and roll the omelets onto a plate.

SERVES 1

Notes

SOUPER

Soups

Soup may be the perfect food — whatever the season or the occasion. Best of all, it's the perfect place to find creative and delicious ways of using those leftovers in your fridge!

Of all the different parts that went into making the Flying Biscuit the magical place it's always been, perhaps nothing was more important than the teamwork that went into it from the very beginning. Delia surrounded herself with creative, talented, and brilliant people, each with her or his own gift. And she also was not afraid to ask friends, and friends of friends, for help. She believed that, deep down, people actually enjoy helping others; she also recognized that she didn't have to try to do everything by herself.

Take the Biscuit's original sign. Wendy said, "I'll do your logo for you," and Delia said, 'Sh—, I didn't even know we needed a logo.'" Delia knew she wanted an angel ("I guess I thought it was going to take a miracle, and I needed as many angels as I could get"). So Wendy hand-painted a delightful angel with beautiful curls and a perfect cherubic face. But Delia noticed something just slightly amiss: "I thought the angel looked so skinny. The way Wendy drew it initially, the angel was like a model from Milan. And it also had a skinny little foot. I asked if she could plump that angel up."

Wendy's spirits flagged—but not for long. It soon became obvious that people were noticing and commenting on the new, full-figured angel that adorned the sign. And in the very first review of the Flying Biscuit, in *Knife and Fork* magazine, noted food critic Christiane Lauterbach made special mention of the sign. She urged readers to pay attention to it before

going inside, because it added so much to the nuances that made the Biscuit stand out. With considerable effort, Delia and the crew wedged the sign up in the window on opening day.

And there it sits to this day. Be sure to take a look the next time you visit.

Tomato Soup with Poached Eggs and Biscuit Croutons

A fast and hearty dinner! This one-pot meal is perfect for a workday supper. For best results, make the tomato soup a day or two ahead, then reheat it. Poach the eggs just before serving.

3 tablespoons olive oil

½ cup minced white onion

1 clove garlic, minced

½ teaspoon crushed red pepper flakes

2 (28-ounce) cans plum tomatoes, with juice

Salt and freshly ground black pepper

3 day-old Famous Flying Biscuits, split and toasted (see page 18)

3 tablespoons unsalted butter

6 large eggs

2 tablespoons basil chiffonade

Freshly grated Parmesan cheese

Heat olive oil in a large saucepan over medium heat. Add onion, reduce the heat to low and saute until golden, about 10 minutes. Add garlic and crushed red pepper flakes and saute for 1 minute more.

Puree tomatoes in a food processor and add to saucepan. Bring to a boil, reduce heat to low and simmer, stirring occasionally, until liquid reduces by a third, about 20 minutes. Add salt and pepper to taste.

Just before serving, cut the biscuits in half and then butter and toast. Crack the eggs into a bowl or cup and slip them one at a time into the simmering soup, distributing them evenly. Cover and cook until the whites are firm but the yolks are still runny, about 8 to 10 minutes.

Distribute the biscuit croutons among six soup bowls. Spoon the eggs onto the tops of the biscuits, then ladle the soup on top. Top each serving with basil and cheese.

SERVES 6

Southern Succotash Soup

A soul food favorite, succotash is taken from the Naragansett Indian word *msickquatash* meaning "boiled whole kernels of corn."

2 tablespoons unsalted butter

3 medium leeks (white and pale green parts only), well washed, drained

¼ cup minced shallots

3 cloves garlic, chopped

2 tablespoons chopped fresh thyme

1 tablespoon chopped fresh oregano

6 tablespoons finely chopped fresh Italian parsley, divided

1 large red bell pepper, seeded and cut into ¼-inch cubes

8 cups chicken stock or canned low-sodium chicken broth

1 ½ cups cooked fresh or thawed frozen baby lima beans

1 (14 ¾-ounce) can creamed corn

1 ½ cups frozen white corn kernels

Salt

In a heavy, large stockpot over medium heat, melt butter. Add leeks, shallots, and garlic; saute until leeks are soft, about 5 minutes.

Add thyme, oregano, and 4 tablespoons parsley; saute about 3 minutes. Stir in bell pepper. Add stock or broth and lima beans and bring to a boil. Reduce heat to medium-low, cover, and simmer until lima beans are tender, about 10 minutes. Add creamed corn and corn kernels and heat through. Remove soup from heat; season with salt to taste. Serve in warmed soup bowls. Top with remaining parsley.

SERVES 6

Butter Bean and Arugula Soup with Parmesan Infusion

A very impressive soup for guests… only you'll know how easy it is.

For Parmesan Infusion:

⅔ cup (packed) grated Parmesan cheese

¼ cup olive oil

For Soup

2 (8-ounce) cans butter beans

2 bay leaves

8 tablespoons olive oil, divided

3 large fresh rosemary sprigs

1 large russet potato, peeled, cut into ½-inch
    pieces (about 2 cups)

10 cloves garlic, chopped and divided

6 cups (or more) chicken stock or canned
    low-sodium chicken broth

Salt and freshly ground black pepper

1 teaspoon dried crushed red pepper

2 bunches arugula, tough stems removed,
    cut into 1-inch strips (about 3 cups)

For Parmesan Infusion

Blend grated Parmesan cheese and olive oil in a food processor until smooth. (Parmesan oil can be prepared the day before. Cover oil and refrigerate.)

For Soup

Rinse butter beans in a colander and place them in a large pot. Pour enough water over beans to cover by 4 inches. Add bay leaves and bring to boil. Reduce heat to medium-low. Add 3 tablespoons olive oil and rosemary sprigs and simmer uncovered until beans are barely tender, about 30 minutes. Remove bay leaves and rosemary sprigs.

Heat 3 tablespoons olive oil in another large pot over medium heat. Add potato pieces and saute until brown in spots, about 8 minutes. Add half the garlic and saute until beginning to color, about 3 minutes. Add 6 cups chicken stock and boil until potato pieces are falling apart, about 10 minutes. Pour beans and cooking liquid into potato mixture. Bring to a boil; reduce heat and simmer about 10 minutes. Season soup with salt and pepper to taste. (Soup can be prepared up to 2 days ahead. To reheat, bring to a simmer, thinning with additional chicken stock if necessary.)

Heat remaining 2 tablespoons olive oil in heavy medium skillet over medium heat. Add remaining garlic and dried crushed red pepper; saute until golden. Add arugula to skillet and wilt; pour into soup and simmer 5 minutes. Stir Parmesan infusion into soup. Season soup to taste with salt and pepper.

SERVES 8 FOR A FIRST COURSE OR 4 FOR A MAIN COURSE

Lettuce and Pea Soup

Wonderful served hot or cold.

2 tablespoons vegetable oil

2 cups chopped white onion

1 head romaine lettuce, sliced (about 5 cups)

6 cups (or more) chicken stock or canned
    low-sodium chicken broth

2 cups cooked fresh or thawed frozen peas

1 ½ teaspoons granulated sugar

1 ½ teaspoons chopped fresh marjoram leaves or
    ¼ teaspoon dried, crumbled

Pinch freshly grated nutmeg

Salt and freshly ground black pepper

¾ cup sour cream

In a large, heavy stockpot, over moderate heat, heat oil. Add onion and saute until softened, about 10 minutes. Stir in romaine and cook, stirring, until lettuce wilts. Stir in stock or broth, peas, sugar, marjoram, nutmeg, and salt and pepper to taste. Simmer soup for 10 minutes.

Puree soup in the stockpot with an immersion blender or in batches with a blender until smooth (use caution when blending hot liquids). Add more broth to thin to desired consistency.

If serving soup hot, return it to stockpot and whisk in sour cream. Heat soup, stirring, just until heated through, but do not let it boil. Serve in warmed soup bowls. If serving soup cold, transfer it to a large bowl and whisk in sour cream. Set bowl in a larger bowl half filled with ice and cold water and cool soup, stirring occasionally for 15 minutes. Serve in chilled soup bowls.

SERVES 6

Hearty Rutabaga Soup

Fun to say... great to eat.

1 tablespoon fine virgin olive oil

2 ½ medium leeks (white and pale green parts only), well washed, drained, and chopped into ½-inch pieces (about 1 ½ cups)

2 stalks celery, chopped into ½-inch pieces (about ½ cup)

1 clove garlic, minced

1 cup (½-inch pieces) peeled turnips (about ½ pound)

1 cup (½-inch pieces) peeled rutabagas (about ½ pound)

1 cup (½-inch pieces) peeled russet potatoes (about ½ pound)

2 cups (½-inch pieces) peeled sweet potatoes (about ½ pound)

6 carrots, sliced into ½-inch coins (about 2 cups)

1 (28-ounce) can diced tomatoes in juice

4 (14 ½-ounce) cans low-sodium vegetable broth, divided

Salt and pepper to taste

In a large, heavy stockpot, over medium-low heat, heat oil. Add leeks, celery, and garlic; saute until vegetables begin to soften, about 5 minutes. Add remaining vegetables, tomatoes, and 2 cans broth and bring to a boil. Reduce heat; cover and simmer until vegetables are very tender, about 45 minutes.

Transfer 4 cups soup to a blender. Puree until almost smooth. Return puree to stockpot. Add remaining broth; bring to a simmer. Season with salt and pepper. Serve in warmed soup bowls.

SERVES 6

I guess sometimes you reach a point where you think, "Wow, that person has done a lot and I don't know if I can ask for much more." I felt that way about Wendy, because she was always helping. And we needed a wine list. So one of my employees did a watercolor for the cover of the wine list. It had been on the table for a week or two, and one day I'm sitting in the office trying to do something, and Wendy comes around the corner and throws that wine list down in front of me and asks, "What is this?" I said, "Well, frankly I didn't feel comfortable asking you for anything else, you've been so kind and you're always helping us." She was so funny, she just said, "You've been cheating on me..." I didn't realize that she would be offended. Wendy really wanted to be the one to do the wine list, and I really didn't get it. And that's the lesson for everyone. When you allow people to help you, it's such a two-way gift.

Potato and Kale Soup

You can substitute any hearty, leafy green for the kale and it's still delicious.

2 teaspoons unsalted butter

2 medium white onions, chopped

1 large clove garlic, minced

1 quart low-sodium vegetable stock

5 cups peeled, cubed boiling potatoes, such as
   round white, round red, or Yukon gold

½ teaspoon dried thyme

¼ teaspoon dry mustard

⅛ teaspoon crushed celery seeds

2 cups whole milk

6 cups chopped kale leaves, ribs removed

¼ teaspoon freshly ground pepper

Kosher salt

In a large stockpot, over medium heat, melt butter. Saute onions and garlic until tender, about 5 minutes. Add vegetable stock, potatoes, thyme, dry mustard, and celery seeds and bring to a boil. Reduce heat and simmer until potatoes are tender, about 15 to 20 minutes.

Remove half of the soup to a food processor and pulse until smooth. Return mixture to stockpot. Add milk, kale, and pepper. Bring back to a boil. Reduce heat and simmer until kale is tender, about 5 minutes. Salt to taste.

SERVES 6

Watermelon and Green Tomato Gazpacho

Fresh and cool… not unlike yourself!

4 cups watermelon, diced and seeded (to save time, use the seedless variety)

2 cups diced green tomatoes

1 cup diced red onion

1 serrano chile, diced

1 cup lime juice, freshly squeezed

1 tablespoon apple cider vinegar

½ cup chopped cilantro

¼ teaspoon white pepper

Salt to taste

1 bottle (16 ounces) sparkling water

In a large bowl or container, mix together all ingredients except the sparkling water and set aside for a least 30 minutes to an hour. (This allows the sweetness of the melon to infuse the green tomatoes.) Spoon the mixture into bowls. Add ⅓ cup sparkling water to each bowl, stir and serve.

SERVES 6

Turkey Tortilla Soup

You will gobble, gobble, gobble it up!

4 teaspoons chili powder

8 cups chicken stock or canned low-sodium
chicken broth

1 (16-ounce) can stewed tomatoes, coarsely
mashed with juices

2 (10-ounce) packages frozen succotash (or 2 cups
each frozen corn and lima beans)

4 cups diced cooked turkey

3 cups coarsely broken corn tortilla chips, divided

4 teaspoons fresh minced or canned jalapeños

Salt and freshly ground pepper

Put chili powder in a heavy medium saucepan. Stir over low heat just until fragrant, about
1 minute. Add stock or broth and tomatoes with juices. Increase heat and bring to a boil. Add
succotash, turkey, ⅓ cup corn chips, and jalapeños. Simmer until vegetables are tender, about
10 minutes. Salt and pepper to taste. Serve in warmed soup bowls. Top with remaining corn chips.

SERVES 6

MR. LEE'S WALK-IN COOLER

The Flying Biscuit's original construction budget wouldn't stretch far enough to allow the purchase of
one very necessary piece of restaurant equipment: a walk-in cooler. Mr. Lee, owner of the neighborhood
grocery across the street, generously allowed Delia to store the Biscuit's refrigerated goods in a space
the width of a tomato box, floor to ceiling, in his beer cooler.

Every evening before the close of business, Biscuit employees would head over to Mr. Lee's Candler
Park Market and pull out the eggs, milk, organic greens, fruit, and produce for the next morning's breakfast rush. But, invariably, as the crowd wound down McLendon Avenue and around Clifton Road on a
busy Saturday morning, the kitchen would find itself short a few essentials. Line cooks would keep a
wary eye out for Mr. Lee's 10 a.m. (ish) arrival, and as soon as his van pulled up in front of the market,
someone would race across the street to grab a few extra tomatoes. Usually, to no one's surprise, the
tomato boxes would be at the bottom of the floor-to-ceiling stack. The kitchen staff grew skilled in the
art of quickly un-piling and re-piling the vertical jigsaw of refrigerated goods. Woe to the line cook who
dropped a carton of eggs, dodging traffic in a rush to cross the street!

Notes

LEFT OF

CENTER

From the beginning, the Flying Biscuit has welcomed all kinds of people to work there and to eat there. It has always been a place that reflects the wonderful diversity of Atlanta. That welcoming and easy-going atmosphere is something Delia knew she wanted the Biscuit to exude. And so it has.

Another ingredient to success has been Delia's high standards for herself and her employees. She expects the most from everyone around her, and she strives to inspire not just a strong work ethic but also a drive for personal growth: "I hope that when you come to work at the Flying Biscuit, your time here will show you that your dreams can come true, that you can create something great for yourself. You have the perfect job waiting for you if you work hard at it and have a goal and always work toward your goal, and never lose track of what you hope for yourself." She believes that jobs in the restaurant industry are a vital and often underappreciated cornerstone of the American economy. In her view, they help build the foundation for what people will go on to do. As Delia puts it, "If you can work in the restaurant industry and do it well and have a great attitude, you'll take that with you forever."

When it comes to setting goals, Delia has for years relied on what she considers a sure-fire method to achieving them: writing her dreams down in a journal. "It doesn't matter if you spell it right, it doesn't matter what you write, it's just about putting in writing all the things that you hope for yourself. There's no wrong. You can't write anything wrong in this." For her, keeping a journal — which she's done since 1992 — was "the only little place in the world where I could just write my biggest dreams, and nobody was going to judge them." Once she took that first tiny step, things began falling into place (including that fateful water main break

on McLendon!). Because it worked for her, she knows that it can work for others, and she is unceasing in encouraging her employees. "If I can do it, anyone can do it" is her mantra, which she shares with those who come to work at the Biscuit, "no matter what their background or education or hurdles they've faced."

Fried Green Tomatoes and Cashew Relish

As featured on *$40 A Day… with Rachael Ray.*

For Cashew Relish

1 ½ cups cashews

2 red jalapeños, stemmed, seeded,
 and roughly chopped

⅓ cup plus additional fresh cilantro leaves
 for garnish

¾ cup honey

⅓ cup white vinegar

For Fried Green Tomatoes

6 cups canola oil

2 ½ cups milk

2 large eggs

1 ½ cups all-purpose flour

½ cup cornmeal

1 tablespoon salt

1 tablespoon celery salt

1 tablespoon black pepper

½ tablespoon cayenne pepper

1 teaspoon onion powder

½ teaspoon paprika

6 medium green tomatoes, sliced ½-inch thick

4 ounces goat cheese, at room temperature

To make Cashew Relish

Combine cashews, jalapeños, and cilantro in a food processor and pulse just until combined. Transfer to a medium bowl. Add honey and vinegar and mix thoroughly; set aside.

To make Fried Green Tomatoes:

Heat the oil in a large, heavy skillet to 375 degrees F. Use a thermometer to make sure the oil doesn't burn or cool. Keep at a constant temperature. (A fry daddy works well too.)

In a medium bowl, combine milk and eggs; set aside.

In another medium bowl, combine flour, cornmeal, salt, celery salt, black pepper, cayenne pepper, onion powder, and paprika.

One at time, dredge tomato slices in flour mixture, then in the egg mixture, then in the flour mixture again.

Fry tomatoes, a few at a time, in the hot oil until golden brown. Drain briefly on paper towels atop a wire rack. While still hot, put three to four tomato slices on each of six plates. Top with goat cheese, Cashew Relish, and extra cilantro leaves.

SERVES 6

Organic Chicken Liver Pâté with Sweet Figs

A French baguette, pâté, and arugula make a great sandwich too!

8 tablespoons unsalted butter, divided

3 large white onions, finely diced

1 pound organic chicken livers, trimmed
  of excess fat (available at health food markets;
  sometimes frozen)

¼ cup tawny port

¼ teaspoon allspice

1 tablespoon fresh lemon juice

Kosher salt and freshly ground black pepper

⅓ cup fig preserves

Toast points, sesame crisps, or toasted baguette

Oil a 1 ½-quart terrine or straight-sided casserole dish and line with plastic wrap; set aside.

In a large, heavy skillet, over moderate heat, melt 2 tablespoons butter. Add onions and cook until soft; transfer them to a food processor. In the same skillet, melt 2 tablespoons butter over moderate heat. Saute chicken livers until they are browned on the outside but still pink inside; transfer them to the food processor.

Add port to the skillet, bring it to a boil, and deglaze the skillet, scraping up the brown bits, for 1 minute. Add the port to the food processor with the remaining butter, allspice, and lemon juice. Puree the mixture until smooth. Add salt and pepper to taste.

Pour the pâté into the prepared terrine, cover with plastic wrap, and refrigerate for 5 hours, or until firm.

To serve, remove plastic wrap from the terrine. Place a serving platter right side down on top of the terrine. Holding the platter tightly to the terrine, flip them over. Remove the terrine; discard the plastic wrap. Smooth the top and sides and spread the preserves on the top. Serve with toast points, crisps, or baguette. The pâté, kept covered and chilled, may be made 4 days in advance.

SERVES 6

Tofu-Stuffed Cabbage Roll-Ups

Roll, roll, roll 'em up.

For Sauce

½ cup (or can) condensed tomato soup

1 (8-ounce) can diced tomatoes

For Roll-Ups

1 scant cup condensed cream of mushroom soup

½ cup (or can) condensed tomato soup

2 (14-ounce) packages firm tofu, drained
 and crumbled*

½ cup finely diced white onion

½ teaspoon ground nutmeg

1 tablespoon salt

½ teaspoon ground black pepper

12 large Savoy cabbage leaves, blanched
 and drained

To make Sauce

In a small mixing bowl, combine tomato soup and diced tomatoes. Pour ⅔ of the mixture into a 9 x 13-inch glass baking dish; set aside.

To make Roll-Ups

Preheat oven to 375 degrees F.

In a large mixing bowl, thoroughly combine mushroom soup, tomato soup, tofu, onion, nutmeg, salt, and pepper.

Lay a cabbage leaf flat. Place 2 tablespoons of the tofu mixture about 1 inch from the end of the leaf. Fold leaf over the mixture, fold left and right edges of the leaf into the center, then tightly roll the leaf into a cylinder, as with a burrito. As they are finished, place each roll into the prepared baking dish. When all 12 rolls are in the baking dish, spread the remaining sauce on top of them.

Cover the dish with foil and bake for 60 to 75 minutes, or until the cabbage rolls are cooked through and the sauce is bubbly.

SERVES 6

*Two pounds of cooked ground turkey can be substituted for the tofu.

Creamy, Dreamy Southern-Style Grits

Our award-winning creamy dreamy grits. Even grit-haters will love these!

6 cups water

2 cups half-and-half

Salt to taste

¼ teaspoon white pepper

2 cups quick grits

½ cup grated sharp white cheddar cheese

4 tablespoons unsalted butter, cubed

In a medium saucepan, combine water, half-and-half, salt, and white pepper and bring to a boil.

Slowly pour grits into boiling water while whisking the entire time. Reduce to low heat and continue to whisk often, until thick and completely smooth, about 10 minutes.

Add white cheddar and allow cheese to melt. Whisk again to combine. Turn heat off and allow grits to rest 5 minutes. Add butter and stir until completely smooth and silky.

SERVES 8

Adzuki Beans and Rice

Adzuki beans are rich in fiber and slightly sweet in flavor.

1 (15-ounce) can adzuki beans, rinsed
   and drained

2 cups green beans, cut into 1-inch pieces

½ cup uncooked brown rice

2 (14-ounce) cans fat-free, reduced-sodium
   chicken or vegetable broth

1 teaspoon ground cumin

1 teaspoon peeled, minced fresh ginger

¼ teaspoon ground turmeric

1 jalapeño pepper, seeded and diced

3 large carrots, thinly sliced

6 plum tomatoes, chopped

Kosher salt and freshly ground black pepper

¼ cup toasted sunflower seeds

In a medium saucepan, over medium heat, combine beans, rice, broth, cumin, ginger, turmeric, jalapeño, and carrots. Bring to a boil, reduce heat and simmer, covered, until rice has expanded and vegetables are tender, about 30 minutes, depending on the type of rice. Add tomatoes. Add salt and pepper to taste and cook for another 5 minutes. Garnish each serving with sunflower seeds.

SERVES 6

Potatoes with Garlic Aioli

French but not fried.

3 pounds medium red potatoes

1 teaspoon plus additional kosher salt

¾ cup extra virgin olive oil, divided

1 tablespoon dried thyme, crumbled

Freshly ground pepper

2 tablespoons mayonnaise

1 ½ tablespoons fresh lemon juice

2 large cloves garlic, smashed

½ tablespoon Dijon mustard

¼ cup vegetable oil

In a large saucepan, cover the potatoes with cold water and 1 teaspoon salt and bring to a boil. Cook over moderate heat until tender, about 15 to 20 minutes. Drain and let cool for 20 minutes. Cut the potatoes in half. Toss with ¼ cup olive oil and thyme. Salt and pepper to taste.

In a food processor, combine mayonnaise, lemon juice, garlic, and mustard. With the machine running, add vegetable oil and remaining olive oil in a thin stream and blend until creamy and emulsified. Cover and chill aioli until ready to serve.

Saute potatoes in a large, heavy saute pan over high heat, turning occasionally, until browned and sizzling, about 10 minutes. Transfer the potatoes to a warm platter and serve with aioli.

SERVES 6

Spicy Wasabi & Sweet Pea Salad with Scallops

East meets southern-style comfort food.

¾ cup packed mint leaves

2 tablespoons fresh lemon juice

½ cup vegetable oil, divided

Salt and freshly ground black pepper

½ pound snow peas, trimmed

½ pound sugar snap peas, snapped

½ pound pea shoots or 2 bunches watercress,
   bottom third of stems removed (4 cups)

2 pounds sea scallops (dry pack)

¼ cup wasabi peas, lightly crushed

In a blender, puree the mint leaves, lemon juice, and 6 tablespoons oil. Season with salt and pepper; set dressing aside.

Fill a medium bowl with ice water; set aside. Bring a medium saucepan of salted water to a boil. Add snow peas and sugar snap peas to the boiling water and cook until bright green and crisp-tender, about 2 minutes. Drain the peas and transfer to the ice water to cool thoroughly; drain and pat dry. Transfer to a large bowl and add the pea shoots or watercress; set aside.

In a large, heavy skillet over high heat, heat the remaining oil. (Oil should shimmer and dance in the pan, but not smoke.) Season scallops with salt and pepper and sear in the skillet until deeply browned on one side, about 3 minutes. Turn the scallops and sear until barely white throughout, about 1 minute.

While scallops cook, toss pea salad with dressing and season with salt and pepper to taste. Transfer the salad to six individual plates. Arrange scallops on top of the pea salad and garnish with a sprinkle of wasabi peas.

SERVES 6

Rocket and Red Lentil Salad

Rocket up a notch.

⅓ cup granulated sugar

2 teaspoons plus additional kosher salt, divided

½ teaspoon plus additional freshly ground pepper

1 large lemon, very thinly sliced

¼ cup plus 2 tablespoons extra virgin olive oil, divided

½ cup couscous

1 cup red lentils

8 ounces rocket lettuce (baby arugula)

1 tablespoon freshly squeezed lemon juice

½ cup shelled unsalted pistachios, toasted and coarsely chopped

In a small saucepan, boil 2 cups water. Add the sugar, 1 ½ teaspoons salt, and ½ teaspoon pepper; stir until the salt dissolves. Add the lemon slices and cook over moderately high heat until softened, about 15 minutes. Transfer the lemon slices to a plate. Boil the liquid until reduced to ⅓ cup, about 3 minutes; let cool. Whisk in ¼ cup oil. (Preserved lemons last up to 2 weeks in the refrigerator. Make extra and ahead of time.)

Bring ¾ cup water to a boil in a saucepan. Add ½ teaspoon salt and the couscous. Remove the pan from the heat, cover, and let stand 5 minutes. Fluff the couscous with a fork.

In a medium saucepan bring 1 quart water to a boil, add the lentils, and cook over moderately high heat until tender, about 8 minutes; drain, transfer to a bowl, and add the couscous.

Stir all but 1 tablespoon of the lemon oil into the couscous and lentils; season. Toss the arugula with the lemon juice and remaining olive oil; season with salt and pepper. Transfer the arugula to plates, mound the couscous on top, and drizzle with the remaining lemon oil. Top with lemon slices and pistachios.

SERVES 6

Tomato and Cornbread Salad

A great use for your summer tomatoes.

1 pound cornbread (not sweet), cut into 1-inch
    cubes (about 6 cups)
½ cup vegetable oil
1 tablespoon fresh oregano
¼ cup rice vinegar
1 ½ teaspoons Dijon mustard
Salt and freshly ground pepper

2 pints cherry tomatoes, halved
2 serrano chiles, cleaned and diced
1 ½ cups grated pepper jack cheese
½ cup coarsely chopped cilantro
1 small red onion, thinly sliced
½ cup toasted shelled pumpkin seeds
Lime wedges

Preheat the oven to 400 degrees F. Toast the cornbread in a single layer on a baking sheet, turning once, until golden.

In a skillet, heat the oil with the oregano over low heat until fragrant, about 8 minutes. Let cool and then strain the oil. In a bowl, whisk the vinegar and mustard. Whisk while you slowly drizzle in the oregano oil. Season with salt and pepper.

In a large bowl, combine the cornbread, tomatoes, serrano chiles, cheese, cilantro, onion, and pumpkin seeds. Add the dressing and toss well. Transfer the salad to plates and serve with lime wedges.

SERVES 6

Spinach and Strawberry Salad

Keep salads fun with this one.

1 bag baby spinach, well rinsed and spun dry

2 pints (4 cups) sliced strawberries

½ cup vegetable oil

¼ cup white wine vinegar

½ cup granulated sugar

¼ teaspoon paprika

2 tablespoons sesame seeds

1 tablespoon poppy seeds

In a large bowl, toss together the spinach and strawberries.

In a medium bowl, whisk together oil, vinegar, sugar, paprika, sesame seeds, and poppy seeds. Pour over the spinach and strawberries, and toss to coat.

SERVES 6

Watermelon and Mint Salad

A sweet summer salad.

1 (5-pound) seedless watermelon

1 large Vidalia or sweet onion

¼ cup red wine vinegar

Salt and pepper

½ cup extra virgin olive oil

2 tablespoons chopped fresh mint

4 ounces feta cheese, crumbled

6 whole mint sprigs, for garnish

Cut rind from melon and cut into bite-size pieces; set aside. Peel and slice the onion into rings.

In a small bowl, combine the vinegar, salt, and pepper, and whisk until salt is dissolved. Slowly drizzle in olive oil while whisking aggressively. Add mint.

In a large bowl, combine melon, onion, and feta cheese. Pour dressing over mixture and toss until everything is coated and evenly mixed. Garnish with whole mint sprigs.

SERVES 6

Apple and Pear Salad

A perfect "pear-ing" for a light salad.

1 head red leaf lettuce

1 head green leaf lettuce

1 teaspoon freshly squeezed lemon juice

2 crisp red apples, such as McIntosh or Gala,
   thinly sliced

2 Anjou pears, thinly sliced

2 tablespoons apple cider

2 tablespoons cider vinegar

1 teaspoon granulated sugar

⅓ cup extra virgin olive oil

Salt and coarsely ground black pepper

8 ounces sharp cheddar cheese, grated

Coarsely chop lettuce. Squeeze lemon juice over apples and pears (to stop them from browning) and toss with greens. Combine cider, vinegar, and sugar in a bowl and whisk in oil in a slow stream. Pour dressing over salad and season salad with salt and pepper. Toss salad to coat evenly and serve with grated cheddar over top.

SERVES 6

Zucchini Capellini

Fun to say, good to eat.

3 medium zucchini, halved and hollowed

2 medium yellow crookneck squash,
   seeds removed

1 teaspoon vegetable oil

¼ teaspoon sesame oil

2 cloves garlic, finely chopped

24 large fresh basil leaves, chiffonaded into
   thin strips

5 teaspoons freshly grated Parmesan cheese

Kosher salt and freshly ground black pepper

Slice the zucchini and yellow squash lengthwise on a mandolin to make very long and thin, noodle-like slices.

In a large nonstick skillet over medium heat, heat oils and brown garlic. Add squash and basil, and gently toss until squash is tender, about 3 minutes. Do not overcook or squash noodles will break apart.

Sprinkle with Parmesan cheese and season with salt and pepper.

SERVES 6

Sugar-Coated Pecans

Nuts are a healthy, delicious snack… and make a great garnish.

1 egg white	¾ teaspoon kosher salt
1 tablespoon water	½ teaspoon ground cinnamon
1 cup granulated sugar	1 pound pecan halves

Preheat oven to 250 degrees F. Butter one large baking sheet and set aside.

In a mixing bowl, whip together the egg white and water until frothy. In a separate bowl, mix together sugar, salt, and cinnamon. Add pecans to egg whites; stir to coat the nuts evenly. Remove nuts with a slotted spoon and toss them in the sugar mixture until coated. Spread nuts on the prepared baking sheet. Bake for 1 hour, stirring every 15 minutes.

MAKES 2 CUPS

MAKE IT HAPPEN!

When in doubt, just make it happen. Work with it. Food is not exact in any way, shape, or form. Half the fun of cooking is trying out new ingredients, new techniques, and new kinds of food. Very few things are inedible. Unless you've made a mistake with salt, most of the time you can fix anything. What's important is to not be afraid, and to make it happen. The same is true when it comes to making biscuits. Everybody makes them differently. Everyone has their own signature and their own handwriting when it comes to cooking food. That's why you should go ahead and do it, because you will make it your own.

Tamari Aioli

A great dipping sauce for veggies… also great on sandwiches!

3 tablespoons peeled fresh ginger

½ tablespoon Dijon mustard

1 tablespoon soy sauce

1 tablespoon rice vinegar

½ teaspoon Tabasco sauce

1 cup mayonnaise

Puree ginger in a food processor until finely chopped. Place chopped ginger in a clean towel and wring the juice into a cup to extract about ½ tablespoon ginger juice.

In a medium mixing bowl, whisk ½ tablespoon ginger juice, mustard, soy sauce, rice vinegar and Tabasco into mayonnaise. Keep refrigerated.

MAKES 1½ CUPS

CENTER

OF PLATE

The Flying Biscuit is more than just a restaurant — it's a state of mind, a way of seeing the world, a community. Still, the food is unforgettably delectable (and not just the biscuits!). Having grown up in the restaurant business, Delia understands the importance of using the freshest and best ingredients. She's also been inspired by the slow food movement, which began in Italy in the 1980s and has become a global phenomenon. It is based on a philosophy that values local growers and traditional methods, small-scale and preferably organic cultivation, and regional cuisine and foodways.

Delia is proud to embrace these ideas at the Biscuit, not only because the end result tastes so good, but also because it has given her the opportunity to work with some amazing people who she might never have known otherwise, like Michael Sabir, founder and president of Tayyib Foods in Atlanta. Sabir, who is Muslim, has been making halal (Islamically acceptable) chicken sausage for nearly two decades. He uses free-range chickens raised in Gainesville, Georgia, as well as natural spices (including a healthy dose of red pepper) and kosher casings. The result is a spicy delight. As Delia tells it, "People eat our chicken sausage and they don't believe that it's just chicken. I think they understand that there's a lot of care in the food, and they feel good about it. Because Michael Sabir puts a lot of care in his sausage, and if I can use as many products as I can where each individual puts a lot of care in his or her product, people come back."

They also come back for the turkey — specifically, the turkeys from Heritage Foods USA, which was founded in 2001. As part of the nonprofit organization Slow Food USA, Heritage Foods is dedicated to preserving small farms and food traditions dating back to the founding of the country.

Their first foray into this field was the Heritage Turkey Project. These turkeys reproduce naturally, live outdoors rather than in small, cramped cages, and are not fed antibiotics, hormones, or animal byproducts. It's good for farmers, it's good for the environment, and it's good for dinner! The turkeys are unsurpassed in taste and quality. As Delia says, "I would rather have a small amount of something that's really, really incredible and great than have a whole bunch of average."

Her search for quality also led her to an enduring relationship with White Lily flour. In her words, "Nothing else will do." It is, hands-down, the finest soft winter wheat flour available, and the biscuits at the Biscuit simply wouldn't fly without it. Founded in Tennessee, White Lily has been the premier self-rising flour in the South for more than a century, and generations of southerners have grown up savoring the mouth-watering delicacies made with a little bit of White Lily and a lot of love. Delia's passion for finding the best ingredients to serve her guests is one of the many reasons Atlantans have been so loyal to the Biscuit for so many years.

Jack Daniel's Espresso Black Bean Chili

A great garnish for our prize-winning chili is a chipotle aioli, a southwestern take on the classic flavored mayonnaise from Provence.

For Chili

32 ounces dried black beans, sorted and rinsed, or 4 (15-ounce) cans black beans

2 tablespoons extra virgin olive oil

2 medium yellow onions, finely chopped

2 tablespoons minced fresh garlic

1 pound Flying Biscuit Signature Free Range Chicken Sausage (ground turkey, chicken, beef, or texturized vegetable protein will also taste great)

3 tablespoons dark chili powder

2 teaspoons ground cumin

1 teaspoon cayenne pepper

¼ cup finely chopped serrano chiles

½ bunch celery, finely chopped

¼ cup brewed espresso

½ cup Jack Daniel's whiskey

1 cup shredded carrots

2 (28-ounce) cans crushed tomatoes

1 tablespoon plus 2 teaspoons kosher salt

½ teaspoon freshly ground black pepper

Cilantro, for garnish

Sour cream, for garnish

For Chipotle Aioli

2 chipotle peppers in adobo sauce

½ tablespoon honey

½ tablespoon balsamic vinegar

1 tablespoon Dijon mustard

1 egg yolk

1 cup extra virgin olive oil

To make Chili

In a 2-quart container, combine beans with enough water to cover by 2 inches. Cover and soak overnight. If using canned beans, skip this step.

In a large stockpot over medium heat, heat oil. Add onions and saute until soft and translucent, about 2 minutes; add garlic and saute until soft, about 2 minutes; add sausage or other protein choice and brown, about 5 minutes.

Drain beans in a colander and rinse under cold running water. Add to the stockpot, followed by all the remaining ingredients. Simmer, stirring often, until beans are tender, about 1½ hours. Add water in 2-cup increments to prevent burning.

To make Chipotle Aioli

Place chipotles, honey, vinegar, mustard, and egg yolk in a food processor or blender. Process on high speed until well blended. With the machine on, add the oil in a slow, steady stream until aioli thickens to the consistency of a thin mayonnaise. Stop the machine when everything is emulsified; scrape down the sides of the container, and pulse to combine. Refrigerate to chill slightly. Garnish chili with aioli, cilantro, and sour cream and serve in warmed soup bowls.

SERVES 6

Chipotles are smoked jalapeño peppers. They come dried or canned in adobo sauce. I prefer the canned version because the sauce gives a great flavor to almost any dish.
Be careful. Chipotles can be very hot!

Simply Fresh Pasta

If you can make biscuits from scratch, you can make fresh pasta too.

6 cups unbleached all-purpose flour, sifted   6 large eggs

Make a mound of flour on a large work surface, form a well in the center, and crack eggs into the well one at time. Lightly beat eggs with a fork in the well, then blend the eggs into the flour with your fingers without letting the eggs run out of the mound. Use a circular motion, knocking flour into the eggs. Knead gently, until the dough comes together. Continue to knead until dough becomes smooth and resilient. Divide dough into 3 portions, cover each with plastic wrap, and allow to rest for 30 minutes.

Lightly flour the work surface and a rolling pin. Press out the dough with the palms of lightly floured hands and begin to spread the dough with the rolling pin. Fold it over and spread it in the opposite direction, continuing the process, until the desired thickness is reached, about 1 millimeter. Lightly sprinkle the sheet of dough with flour and loosely roll it up, jellyroll-style. Cut with a sharp knife into strips, about ¼-inch wide for tagliatelle, ⅜ inch for fettuccine or ½ inch for pappardelle.

Unroll the pasta strips and spread them on a lightly floured surface to dry for at least 1 hour. Pasta is ready to boil and top with your favorite sauce! Always cook pasta in abundant boiling, salted water. Once you drop your pasta into the boiling water, do not leave the pasta's side! Stir gently for about 3 minutes. The pasta is done when it floats to the top of the water, but take a piece out and try it to be sure it is just right.

SERVES 6

Aunt Millie Romano's Spaghetti alla Carbonara

Steeped in Italian tradition. Turkey bacon is substituted for the usual pancetta.

1½ pounds dried spaghetti

3 large egg yolks

¾ cup heavy cream

1 tablespoon extra virgin olive oil

6 ounces turkey bacon cut into ⅛-inch dice

3 cloves garlic, chopped

Pinch of freshly grated nutmeg

1 cup freshly grated Parmesan or pecorino cheese, plus more for garnish

Freshly ground black pepper

In a large stockpot, boil 6 quarts of water with 2 tablespoons salt. Cook the spaghetti al dente (firm to the tooth), about 6 minutes. Reserve ¾ cup of the pasta cooking water, then drain the pasta. Do not rinse.

In a small bowl, whisk egg yolks and cream; set aside. In a large, deep nonstick saute pan over medium heat, heat oil. Add turkey bacon and cook, stirring frequently, until crisp. Add garlic and cook until golden brown.

Add pasta to skillet. Cook over low heat, tossing, until coated. Slowly add reserved pasta cooking water and cream mixture. Toss over medium heat until eggs are set, about 1 minute. Add nutmeg and 1 cup cheese and toss to coat. Season with pepper to taste and toss a few more times. Serve with extra cheese.

SERVES 6

WRITE IT DOWN!

Be sure to write in this cookbook — your notes, your thoughts, everything. Recipes are passed down as a form of family history. I love to see a recipe that my grandmother wrote on. The cookbook is to be passed down, and it's important to have your handwriting in there. Write in it, use it.

Tommy Champion's Spaghetti and Crabs

A traditional family recipe… as kids, we referred to all pasta as spaghetti, but angel hair or capellini work best in this dish.

12 live (medium-size) blue crabs
2 tablespoons extra virgin olive oil
1 clove garlic, diced
½ tablespoon crushed red pepper flakes

1 (28-ounce) can peeled diced tomatoes,
  with juice
Kosher salt and freshly ground black pepper
16 ounces angel hair pasta

To clean crabs, blanch live crabs in boiling, salted water for 1 minute. Drain crabs in a colander, rinse shells under cool water, pull back the apron, and remove with a twist. The gills and organs should be discarded; the orange-colored roe is edible and delicious.

In a deep stockpot over medium heat, heat olive oil. Add garlic and crushed red pepper flakes. Add crabs and saute for 1½ minutes per side. Add tomatoes, salt, and pepper. Simmer 1½ hours. Cook pasta in salted water until al dente. Drain and toss into sauce. Place spaghetti in warmed serving bowls and garnish with the crabs.

SERVES 6

For some extra fun, cover your dining table in newspaper. When pasta is served, use your fingers to grab the crabs and discard the shells on the newspaper. Make a mess and enjoy!

Fettucine with Smoked Salmon and Sweet Peas

Pasta with fish? That's dee-lish!

2 tablespoons unsalted butter
½ cup heavy cream
8 ounces frozen peas

16 ounces fresh or dried fettuccine
8 ounces smoked salmon, diced
Kosher salt and freshly ground black pepper

In a large skillet over medium heat, melt butter. Add cream and bring to a boil. Stir in peas. Cook until tender and mixture has reduced by one-third.

Cook fettuccine in salted water until al dente. Drain well and pour into cream sauce. Toss to coat pasta. Add smoked salmon to pasta and toss again. Salt and pepper to taste.

SERVES 6

A DISHWASHER'S STORY

Today, the Candler Park Flying Biscuit has two dining rooms, a patio, full-sized kitchen, coffee bar, and even a bakery with its own separate entrance. But back in 1994, the Biscuit's burgeoning business was bursting the seams of Delia's original 900-square-foot space.

Once cooks Jesse, Annie, and dishwasher Frankie joined Delia on the line each morning, there was no getting off the line. They squeezed themselves into places at the sink and gas range, with the biscuits warming under lights, at their backs. Frankie — wedged between a tiny window and a four-compartment sink — feverishly washed and rinsed dishes. As each batch was ready, he'd yell, "Glasses!" up the line. Jesse would suspend work on a sun-dried tomato and goat cheese omelet, Annie would stop flipping Love Cakes and elbow Delia: "Psst — glasses." They would all suck in their stomachs and lean over the griddle, while Frankie shimmied past with stacks and stacks of glass racks.

Frankie and the ladies of the line repeated this process, all morning long, day after day, for each batch of spoons, forks, plates, knives, coffee cups, and orange juice tumblers. True to form and ever able to see the bright side, Delia looks back and thinks, well, at least Frankie had a window...

Catfish with Pecan Brown Butter

Firm, sweet and juicy... it's purrfect.

6 tablespoons unsalted butter, divided
6 (6-ounce) catfish fillets
Salt and freshly ground black pepper
Cayenne pepper

⅓ cup all-purpose flour
½ cup toasted pecan pieces
2 teaspoons fresh lemon juice
Finely grated zest of 1 lemon

In a large nonstick skillet over medium-high heat, melt 2 tablespoons butter. Season both sides of each fillet with salt, pepper, and a pinch of cayenne pepper. Lightly dredge catfish fillets in flour, then add them to the skillet and cook until golden brown and cooked through, about 10 minutes. Transfer fillets to a heatproof plate and cover with foil to keep warm.

Melt remaining butter in the skillet over medium-high heat. Add pecans and cook until the butter and pecans are browned. (This can happen fast so don't blink!) Stir in the lemon juice and zest and salt to taste. Spoon pecans and butter over catfish fillets; serve immediately.

SERVES 6

Flyin' Shrimp and Grits

True Grit style.

1 tablespoon olive oil

2 cloves garlic, minced

½ cup diced onion

½ cup diced celery

½ cup diced carrots

1 can (14½ ounces) diced tomatoes

½ teaspoon Tabasco sauce

¼ teaspoon Worcestershire sauce

¼ cup diced roasted red peppers

¼ teaspoon paprika

¼ teaspoon crushed red pepper flakes

¼ cup basil, chiffonade

¼ teaspoon black pepper

Salt to taste

2 pounds shrimp, peeled and de-veined, tails left on

Creamy, Dreamy Southern-Style Grits (see page 70)

Heat olive oil in a deep saute pan over medium heat. Add garlic, onion, celery, and carrots and cook until tender. Add tomatoes, Tabasco, Worcestershire, roasted red peppers, paprika, crushed red pepper flakes, basil, black pepper and salt. Stir to incorporate spices and simmer 20 to 30 minutes.

Add shrimp and continue to cook over medium heat, about 4 minutes, until shrimp are pink and the tails curl. Do not leave the shrimps' side as they are best if they are not over cooked! Ladle over Creamy, Dreamy Southern-Style Grits.

SERVES 6

Clifford Cook's Salmon Cakes

Serve 'em up hot for breakfast, lunch, or dinner.

2 pounds salmon fillets

½ tablespoon kosher salt

½ teaspoon freshly ground black pepper

5 large eggs

2 cups mayonnaise

1 small red bell pepper, seeded and diced
   (about ½ cup)

1 small green bell pepper, seeded and diced
   (about ½ cup)

1 small white onion, diced (about ½ cup)

4 cups panko bread crumbs

1 tablespoon chopped fresh dill

1 tablespoon dried yellow mustard

1 tablespoon unsalted butter

2 tablespoons extra virgin olive oil

Preheat oven to 350 degrees F. Line a sheet pan with parchment paper.

Place the salmon on the prepared sheet pan and season with salt and pepper. Bake for 8 to 10 minutes. Allow the salmon to cool before flaking into a large mixing bowl.

In a small bowl, whisk the eggs. Add eggs to the flaked salmon with the mayonnaise, bell peppers, onion, bread crumbs, dill, and mustard. Mix well. Portion the mixture into 12 patties. In a large nonstick saute pan over medium heat, melt butter and heat olive oil. Saute patties for approximately 3 to 4 minutes per side, or until brown and crisp.

SERVES 6

Stir-Fried Tofu with 'Shrooms, Sugar Snaps, and Snow Peas

Say that ten times fast!

3 tablespoons dark soy sauce

1 tablespoon unseasoned rice vinegar

1 tablespoon honey

1 teaspoon sesame oil

¼ teaspoon crushed red pepper flakes

1 (12-ounce) package extra-firm tofu, drained, pressed, patted dry, and cut into ½-inch cubes

¼ cup water

1 teaspoon cornstarch

2 tablespoons vegetable oil, divided

1 tablespoon peeled, minced fresh ginger

4 cloves garlic, minced

6 ounces fresh shiitake mushrooms, stemmed and caps quartered

4 ounces sugar snap peas, trimmed

4 ounces snow peas, strings removed

1 baby bok choy, quartered

Kosher salt and freshly ground black pepper

In a medium bowl, blend soy sauce, vinegar, honey, sesame oil, and red pepper flakes. Add tofu and gently stir to coat; set aside to marinate 30 minutes. Remove tofu and set aside remaining marinade. Whisk together water and cornstarch, then add to marinade.

In a large nonstick skillet over medium-high heat, heat 1 tablespoon vegetable oil. Add tofu and saute until golden brown, about 2 minutes. Transfer tofu to a plate.

Add remaining 1 tablespoon oil to skillet. Add ginger and garlic and stir about 1 minute. Add mushrooms and stir-fry until tender, about 3 minutes. Add peas and bok choy and stir-fry until tender, about 3 minutes. Return tofu to skillet and drizzle reserved marinade mixture on top. Stir-fry until marinade thickens slightly, about 30 seconds. Add salt and pepper to taste.

SERVES 4

Tuna Burger with Chimichurri Herb Sauce

Chimichurri is a popular sauce from Argentina. It's great for all grilled meats.

For Chimichurri Herb Sauce

½ cup chopped flat-leaf parsley

½ cup extra virgin olive oil

4 cloves garlic, diced

2 tablespoons sherry vinegar

½ teaspoon dried cumin

1 teaspoon cayenne pepper

½ teaspoon kosher salt

½ teaspoon black pepper

For Tuna Burgers

1 ½ pounds sushi-grade tuna

1 tablespoon extra virgin olive oil

¼ teaspoon cayenne pepper

Kosher salt and freshly ground black pepper

4 Kaiser rolls

To make Chimichurri Herb Sauce

In a medium bowl, combine all ingredients and chill overnight. Bring to room temperature before serving.

To make Tuna Burgers

In a food processor, pulse together tuna, olive oil, and cayenne pepper until mixture loosely holds together. Add salt and pepper to taste. Form into 4 patties, at least 1-inch thick and then chill for at least 1 hour.

On an oiled grill over medium heat, cook burgers for 4 to 5 minutes on each side. Place each on a Kaiser roll, and serve with Chimichurri Herb Sauce.

SERVES 4

Vegetable Cobbler

Short on meat… long on flavor.

For Filling

3 tablespoons unsalted butter, divided

1 large onion, chopped

2 large stalks celery, diced

1 ½ pounds new red potatoes, cut in half

1 medium turnip, peeled and cut into
    ½-inch pieces

1 large carrot, peeled and cut into ½-inch pieces

2 cups frozen peas

8 ounces fresh shiitake mushrooms, stemmed
    and caps diced

¼ cup chopped fresh chives

1 ½ teaspoons crumbled, dried thyme

¾ teaspoon ground cumin

½ teaspoon ground black pepper

¼ teaspoon cayenne pepper

Salt

1 (14-ounce) can vegetable broth

1 cup water

1 cup whipping cream

1 tablespoon all-purpose flour

For Cobbler Crust

2 cups all-purpose flour

1 tablespoon double-acting baking powder

1 teaspoon salt

¼ cup chopped fresh chives

6 tablespoons chilled and unsalted butter,
    cut into ½-inch pieces

2 large eggs

½ cup whole milk

To make Filling

In a heavy stockpot, melt 2 tablespoons butter over medium-high heat. Add onion and celery and saute until tender and golden. Add potatoes, turnip, carrot, peas, mushrooms, chives, thyme, cumin, black pepper, cayenne pepper, and salt; stir well. Add vegetable broth and water and bring to a strong simmer, cover and cook until all vegetables are barely tender, about 15 to 20 minutes. Stir in cream. Season with salt to taste.

Mix remaining butter and flour in a small bowl to blend. Stir into stew and continue to simmer until it thickens slightly, about 5 to 10 minutes. Ladle stew into six ramekins.

To make Cobbler Crust

Preheat oven to 425 degrees F. Line a large sheet pan with parchment paper.

Sift flour, baking powder, and salt into a bowl. Stir in chives. Add butter and rub in with fingertips until mixture resembles coarse meal. Add eggs and milk and stir until soft moist dough forms.

Turn dough out onto generously floured surface. Knead gently just to combine. Divide dough into 6 equal pieces; pat out each piece to a 3½-inch round. Place 1 dough round atop vegetable filling in each ovenproof dish. Place dishes on sheet pan. Bake until topping is golden and vegetable mixture is heated through, about 18 to 22 minutes.

SERVES 6

Ostrich Fan Fillets

Ostrich is low in fat... high in protein.

2 cups balsamic vinegar

2 tablespoons granulated sugar

1 ½ teaspoons crushed black
   peppercorns

6 (6-ounce) ostrich fillets

1 teaspoon kosher salt, divided

Place vinegar and sugar in a small heavy saucepan over medium heat. Heat to a simmer and reduce by half. Remove from heat and cool. Rub peppercorns onto both sides of ostrich fillets. Sprinkle with ½ teaspoon salt and allow fillets to stand 15 to 30 minutes.
Preheat oven to 250 degrees F.

Heat a cast-iron skillet over high heat, sprinkle in ½ teaspoon salt, and wait until the salt begins to smoke. Sear fillets 1 minute per side and then place skillet in the oven with a piece of foil loosely over the meat. Leave for 10 to 15 minutes. Meat will become evenly pink inside. Drizzle about 1 ounce of the balsamic reduction over fillets.

SERVES 6

Braised Chicken Thighs with Herb Potatoes

This recipe can be prepared in an electric slow cooker or crock-pot too.

8 chicken thighs, about 2 pounds

2 tablespoons all-purpose flour

3 teaspoons Hungarian paprika

1 teaspoon kosher salt

½ teaspoon black pepper

1 teaspoon fresh thyme

1 teaspoon fresh oregano

1 teaspoon extra virgin olive oil

2 cups sliced carrots

1 large onion, diced

2 cups fat-free, low-sodium chicken broth

½ cup white wine

1 ½ pounds small, round red potatoes, halved

In a large ziplock plastic bag, add chicken, flour, paprika, salt, pepper, thyme, and oregano. Seal bag and shake, shake, shake to coat chicken. Set bag in a medium bowl and marinate 30 minutes.

In a Dutch oven over medium heat, heat oil, and then add chicken and marinade. Brown chicken on both sides. Add carrots and onion; stir to coat. Add broth, wine, and potatoes, and bring to a boil. Reduce heat and simmer 45 minutes to 1 hour, or until chicken and vegetables are tender.

SERVES 4

Chili con Tofu with Cheddar and Jalapeño Biscuits

A twist on a classic.

2 large onions, chopped (about 3 cups)

¼ cup vegetable oil

1 tablespoon minced garlic

2 carrots, peeled and thinly sliced

2 (12- to 16-ounce) packages firm tofu,
  cut into ½-inch cubes

¼ cup chili powder

1 tablespoon ground cumin

2 tablespoons paprika

1 tablespoon crumbled, dried oregano

1 tablespoon dried hot red pepper flakes,
  or to taste

2 (8-ounce) cans tomato sauce

4 cups vegetable broth

3 tablespoons cider vinegar

1 (19-ounce) can kidney beans, rinsed
  and drained

2 green bell peppers, chopped

Salt and freshly ground black pepper

Cheddar and Jalapeño Biscuits (see page 21)

In a stockpot, cook onions in oil over moderately low heat, stirring occasionally, until they are soft. Add garlic and carrots and cook the mixture, stirring, for 1 minute.

Add tofu, chili powder, cumin, paprika, oregano, and red pepper flakes and cook mixture, stirring, for 5 minutes. Add tomato sauce, broth, and vinegar. Bring the mixture to a boil, and simmer it, covered, stirring occasionally, for 20 minutes. Add kidney beans, bell peppers, and salt and black pepper to taste. Simmer the mixture, uncovered, for 15 minutes.

Arrange a Cheddar and Jalapeño Biscuit, heated and split, on each of six dinner plates, spoon chili over the bottom half, and cover it with the top half of the biscuit.

SERVES 6 PLUS ADDITIONAL FOR LEFTOVERS

Ginger Crab Cakes

Sorry Mary Ann. This li'l buddy only needs ginger!

1 pound crabmeat (peekytoe and lump)
½ cup mayonnaise
2 tablespoons chopped cilantro
1 tablespoon fresh lime juice
4 teaspoons peeled fresh minced ginger
¼ teaspoon diced serrano chiles
¼ teaspoon Tabasco sauce

¼ teaspoon salt
¼ teaspoon black pepper
2 large eggs
¾ cup panko bread crumbs
¼ cup canola oil
Tamari Aioli (see page 81)

In a large bowl, mix crabmeat, mayonnaise, cilantro, lime juice, ginger, serranos, Tabasco, salt and pepper. Shape into 12 cakes.

In a shallow dish, beat eggs and in another shallow dish, place bread crumbs. Dip crab cakes into egg, then press into bread crumbs to coat.

In a large heavy-bottomed skillet, heat canola oil over medium-high heat; shimmering but not smoking! Saute crab cakes about 3 minutes per side until crisp and browned. Serve on a puddle of Tamari Aioli.

MAKES 6 BIGGIE CAKES

Notes

HAPPY

ENDINGS

Or is it happy beginnings? In 2006, Delia joined with Raving Brands to franchise the Flying Biscuit. Now you won't have to be in Atlanta to enjoy a little "biscuit love." As she has ever since she founded the Biscuit, Delia is once again surrounding herself with a talented team — people who share her dream of bringing the Flying Biscuit's special southern-funky-vibe and mouthwatering food to cities beyond Atlanta and the South.

Will each new Flying Biscuit be a cookie-cutter replica of the original? Not a chance! The beauty of the Biscuit lies in its special connection to neighborhoods and communities. The Midtown Atlanta store has its own feel, its own rhythm, which comes from the people who live and work in the bustling heart of the city, just as the Candler Park location has its own special atmosphere. The idea is not to merely imitate what's already been done, but to create new spaces that reflect the uniqueness of a particular region, city, and neighborhood. The same principles that Delia has held onto for all these years are evident in this new chapter of the Flying Biscuit's story: having a dream (and writing it down!), sharing the dream, a lot of hard work, and a whole lot of love.

Delia has what she likes to call a "When I'm eighty" story, and it's about taking chances and living without regret. When she was first trying to get the restaurant open, she called an attorney (the father of a friend) and asked for advice. But all he did was tell her that most restaurants fail and that she probably would too. "He just went down the list: 'Have you done that, have you done this, do you know this?' and most of my answers frankly were no. By the end he said, 'Who do you think you are, that you think you can open a restaurant? Who do

you think you are?' I hung up that phone and I just started crying. His words were ringing in my head. You're right, who do I think I am? But then I just said, 'You know what? I will regret if I don't try this. When I am eighty years old and I sit in that rocking chair and I look back at my life, I will regret that at this moment I let that stranger on the other end of that phone stop me from trying. And if I fail, I will not regret failing. I will not regret paying my debts. I will regret not trying.'" What will you try? Who do you think you are?

Chocolate Biscuit Bread Pudding with Honey Crème Anglaise

The ultimate comfort food at the Flying Biscuit Cafe.

For Honey Crème Anglaise

4 large egg yolks

½ cup granulated sugar

2 cups heavy cream

2 tablespoons honey

For Bread Pudding

3 cups heavy cream

1 cup whole milk

1 pound semisweet chocolate, chopped into small bits

1 cup granulated sugar

12 large egg yolks

1 teaspoon pure vanilla extract

10 Flying Biscuits, day-old, and crumbled into bite-size pieces (see page 18)

Sprig of mint

To make Honey Crème Anglaise

Whisk together egg yolks and sugar in a small bowl until smooth and light in color.

In a small saucepan over medium heat, bring cream to a simmer. Remove from heat.

Whisk ½ cup hot cream into egg yolk mixture until thoroughly combined. Whisk all of the tempered egg yolk mixture back into the remaining cream in the saucepan and return to medium heat. Cook, stirring continuously with a wooden spoon, until cream coats the back of the spoon. Remove from stove and stir in honey. Transfer to a glass or ceramic bowl and chill until ready to serve. Serve cold.

To make Bread Pudding

Combine cream and milk in a large heavy saucepan. Bring to a simmer over medium heat. Remove from heat and whisk in chocolate. Once the chocolate has melted and is thoroughly combined, set aside.

In a medium mixing bowl, whisk together sugar, egg yolks, and vanilla. Whisk 1 cup of the warm chocolate mixture to the egg yolk mixture until thoroughly combined. Whisk all of the tempered egg yolk mixture into the remaining chocolate and cream mixture in the saucepan until thoroughly combined.

Arrange crumbled biscuits into the bottom of a 12 x 9 ½-inch metal baking pan. Pour the chocolate custard over the biscuits. Make sure the biscuits are submerged in the chocolate custard. Let soak for 30 minutes.

Position rack in middle of oven. Preheat oven to 350 degrees F.

Set the metal pan into a 13 x 9 x 2-inch glass baking pan, filled with enough warm water to measure halfway up the side of the metal pan. Place the pans on the center rack in the oven. Bake in this water bath for 40 to 45 minutes. Custard will be just set when done.

Remove pudding from water bath and cool in the pan on a wire rack for 20 minutes, cut into rectangles. Pour a small puddle of Honey Crème Anglaise onto dessert plates, place serving of pudding on each plate, and drizzle top with more sauce. Garnish with a sprig of mint.

SERVES 6

Chocolate-Hazelnut Biscotti

A crisp biscotti is a good biscotti.

1 cup hazelnuts
4 ½ cups all-purpose flour
1 tablespoon double-acting baking powder
½ teaspoon salt
2 sticks (½ pound) unsalted butter,
    at room temperature

1 ½ cups sugar
4 large eggs
1 tablespoon pure vanilla extract
5 ½ ounces bittersweet chocolate, cut into ½-inch
    chunks (about 1 cup)

Position rack in middle of oven. Preheat oven to 400 degrees F.

Spread hazelnuts on an ungreased sheet pan and bake until golden brown, about 8 minutes. Remove from oven and let nuts cool, then coarsely chop and set aside.

In a medium bowl, sift together flour, baking powder, and salt.

In a large bowl, cream together butter and sugar. Beat in eggs, one at a time, blending thoroughly after each addition. Stir in vanilla. Gradually stir in flour, one cup at a time, blending thoroughly after each addition. Fold in nuts and chocolate until just blended.

Divide dough into 4 equal portions and shape each piece into a 12-inch log. Set the logs on two lightly buttered sheet pans and cover loosely with plastic wrap. Refrigerate until chilled, at least 30 minutes.

Preheat oven to 325 degrees F.

Bake the dough logs until they are firm and starting to brown, about 20 minutes. Transfer the logs to a wire rack and let cool until they can be handled easily, about 5 minutes. Lower oven temperature to 250 degrees F. Using a serrated knife, cut the logs crosswise diagonally into cookies ½ inch thick. Set the cookies on their side on ungreased sheet pans and bake for 15 minutes, or until golden brown. Let cool completely on wire rack before serving.

MAKES 4 DOZEN

Banana Empanadas with Chocolate Gravy

Mary Bell and Jose Luis brought this recipe to the Biscuit from Acapulco. Masa de harina is readily available in chain supermarkets; if not, look for Quaker Oats and Maseca brands in health food or Mexican groceries.

For Empanada Dough

1 1/2 cups all-purpose flour

1 cup masa de harina

1 teaspoon baking powder

1 teaspoon salt

1/2 cup unsalted butter, melted and cooled

1 large egg beaten with 1 tablespoon water

For Empanada Filling

4 large ripe bananas

2 tablespoons granulated sugar

1 teaspoon cinnamon

4 ounces semisweet chocolate, broken into 20 chunks

For Chocolate Gravy

5 heaping tablespoons Hershey's cocoa

1 heaping cup granulated sugar

1 heaping cup all-purpose flour

1 cup water

Confectioners' sugar (for garnish)

To make Empanada Dough

In a large bowl, sift together the flour, masa de harina, baking powder, and salt. Stir in melted butter. Gradually add ½ to ¾ cup of water, working it in with your hands to incorporate; the dough should hold together well but not be sticky. Form the dough into 2 balls of equal size, wrap each separately in plastic wrap, and chill for 30 minutes.

To make Empanada Filling

In a medium bowl, mash bananas, sugar, and cinnamon together until creamy, yet slightly chunky; cover with plastic wrap and set aside.

To make Empanadas

Unwrap 1 ball of dough onto a lightly floured surface. With a lightly floured rolling pin, roll out to a thickness of ⅛ inch. Using a 4-inch cookie or biscuit cutter dipped in flour, cut out 10 circles of dough, placing each on a sheet pan; repeat with remaining ball of dough.

Spoon a generous tablespoon of filling into the center of each pastry circle, leaving a ½-inch border. Place a piece of chocolate on top of the filling. Brush the edges of the pastry circle with the egg and water mixture and then fold the pastry in half to enclose the filling and form a semicircle. Tightly seal the edges by crimping with the tines of a fork. Cover sheet pan loosely with plastic wrap and chill at least 30 minutes before baking.

Position rack in middle of oven. Preheat oven to 375 degrees F.

Transfer the empanadas to a buttered sheet pan and brush the tops with remaining egg and water mixture. Using a fork, prick a few holes in the top of the empanadas to allow steam to escape. Bake for 30 minutes, or until the pastry is golden brown. Serve immediately, drizzled with Chocolate Gravy and dusted with confectioners' sugar.

To make Chocolate Gravy

In a medium bowl, mix together cocoa, sugar, flour, and water. Pour mixture into a medium saucepan and bring to a boil over high heat. Reduce heat to medium and stir constantly, to keep from sticking, until thickened. Drizzle over hot banana empanadas… or almost anything!

SERVES 4 TO 6

~~Strawberry~~ *Rasberry* Rhubarb Cobbler with Cornmeal Biscuit Topping

This cobbler is a gobbler!

For Filling

½ cup granulated sugar

2 tablespoons all-purpose flour

⅛ teaspoon ground cloves

2 (12-ounce) baskets ~~strawberries~~ *Rasberry*, hulled and halved

12 ounces fresh or frozen rhubarb, cut into ½-inch slices (about 2 cups)

For Topping

1 cup all-purpose flour

⅓ cup granulated sugar

¼ cup yellow cornmeal

1 tablespoon baking powder

1 teaspoon baking soda

⅛ teaspoon salt

3 tablespoons unsalted butter, chilled and cut into ½-inch cubes

½ cup low-fat buttermilk

½ cup Honey Crème Anglaise (see page 108)

To make Filling

In a large bowl, mix together sugar, flour, and cloves. Add strawberries and rhubarb, and toss to coat with sugar mixture. Transfer filling to a 10-inch diameter glass pie plate.

To make Topping

Position rack in middle of oven. Preheat oven to 400 degrees F.

In a medium bowl, mix together flour, sugar, cornmeal, baking powder, baking soda, and salt. Work butter into the dry mix with a pastry cutter or your fingers until mixture resembles coarse meal. Add buttermilk, and mix until moist sticky clumps form. Do not over mix. Drop by heaping tablespoon evenly over filling. Bake until filling is bubbly and tender and topping is golden brown, about 25 minutes. Serve warm with a drizzle of Honey Crème Anglaise.

SERVES 6

Lemon Blueberry Cobbler

Blueberries are a power food… so be sure to get a big piece!

1 pint (2 cups) blueberries, washed and
    picked over
1 teaspoon freshly grated lemon zest
⅓ cup granulated sugar
1 tablespoon freshly squeezed lemon juice
1 teaspoon cornstarch

⅔ cup all-purpose flour
1 teaspoon baking powder
⅛ teaspoon ground cardamom
⅛ teaspoon salt
½ cup heavy cream

Position rack in middle of oven. Preheat oven to 400 degrees F. Butter an 8-inch-diameter (1 ½-quart) glass pie plate.

In a medium bowl, toss together blueberries, zest, sugar, lemon juice, and cornstarch until combined well; transfer to prepared pie plate.

In another medium bowl, sift together flour, baking powder, cardamom, and salt. Add cream and stir just until mixture forms a dough. Drop dough in 5 mounds on blueberry mixture. Bake in middle of oven until filling is bubbly and cooked through and dough is golden brown, about 25 minutes.

SERVES 6

Very Berry Crumble

Use any combination of berries you like—blueberries, raspberries, blackberries, and strawberries all work well.

¼ cup plus 2 tablespoons packed light brown sugar, divided

¼ cup all-purpose flour

¼ cup rolled oats

¼ teaspoon cinnamon

⅛ teaspoon salt

2 tablespoons unsalted butter, chilled and cut into ½-inch pieces

¼ cup toasted pecan pieces

2 pints mixed fresh berries, washed and picked over

2 tablespoons freshly squeezed lemon juice

1 tablespoon cornstarch

¼ teaspoon finely grated fresh ginger

1 pint ice cream (optional)

Position rack in middle of oven. Preheat oven to 400 degrees F.

In a medium bowl, combine ¼ cup brown sugar, flour, oats, cinnamon, and salt. Using a pastry cutter or your fingers, work in butter until mixture forms pea-sized lumps. Add pecans and mix lightly just to combine.

In a large bowl, toss together berries, lemon juice, cornstarch, ginger, and remaining brown sugar. In an 8 x 8-inch baking dish, pour half the berry mixture. Sprinkle half the crumble mixture on top of the berries. Add remaining berries, then sprinkle the remaining crumble mixture on top of the berries. Bake until filling is bubbling and top is golden brown, about 25 minutes. Serve warm with ice cream, if desired.

SERVES 6

Lemon Pudding Cake

A very light finish to compliment a hearty meal.

¼ cup unsalted butter, melted and cooled

1 cup granulated sugar, divided

3 large eggs, separated, at room temperature

¼ cup unbleached all-purpose flour

¼ plus ⅛ teaspoon salt

1 ¼ cups whole milk, at room temperature

⅓ cup freshly squeezed lemon juice,
   at room temperature

1 tablespoon finely grated lemon zest

Whipped cream (optional)

Position rack in the middle of oven. Preheat oven to 350 degrees F. Butter an 8 ½ x 8 ½ x 2-inch baking dish.

In a large bowl, whisk butter, ⅔ cup sugar, and egg yolks until smooth and light, about 1 minute. Add flour and salt and pour in just enough milk to whisk the flour smoothly into the egg yolk mixture. When smooth, whisk in the remaining milk and lemon juice until smooth. The mixture should be very fluid.

With an electric mixer on medium speed, beat the egg whites in a large bowl until foamy, about 1 minute. Increase mixer speed to high and beat just until the whites hold soft peaks when the beaters are pulled away, about 2 minutes. Reduce mixer speed to medium. With mixer running, very slowly sprinkle in the remaining sugar; this should take about 1 minute. Stop the mixer and scrape the bowl. Beat on high speed until the whites hold firm peaks.

Add one-third of the egg whites and lemon zest to egg yolk mixture and whisk until combined. Gently incorporate the remaining whites into the batter, using the whisk in a folding/stirring motion. The batter will still be thin. Pour the batter evenly into prepared baking dish. Place baking dish in a 13 x 9 x 2-inch baking dish, filled with enough warm water to measure halfway up the side of the smaller baking dish, and place the dishes on the center rack in the oven. Bake 25 to 30 minutes, or until top of cake is light golden and springs back after gentle pressure. Remove from oven and cool to room temperature on a wire rack. Refrigerate at least 2 hours. Serve with whipped cream, if desired.

SERVES 6 TO 8

Apple and Spice Upside-Down Cake

Sugar 'n' spice 'n' everything nice.

For Topping

3 tablespoons unsalted butter

½ cup packed light brown sugar

1 pound Granny Smith apples, peeled, cored,
  and cut into thin wedges

For Cake

1 cup all-purpose flour

¼ cup granulated sugar

1 teaspoon double-acting baking powder

½ teaspoon baking soda

½ teaspoon salt

½ teaspoon cinnamon

5 tablespoons unsalted butter, cold and cut into
  ½-inch pieces

½ cup buttermilk, well shaken

½ cup crème fraîche or sour cream (optional)

To make Topping

In a 10-inch cast iron or other heavy skillet, over moderate heat, heat butter until foam subsides. Stir in brown sugar and remove from heat. Spread mixture evenly in skillet and arrange apple wedges in one circular layer with edges overlapping slightly.

To make Cake

Position rack in middle of oven. Preheat oven to 425 degrees F.

In a food processor, pulse together flour, sugar, baking powder, baking soda, salt, and cinnamon. Add butter and pulse until mixture resembles coarse meal. Transfer to a large bowl and add buttermilk, stirring just until mixture is moistened. Gently drop batter on top of apples and gently spread into an even layer, leaving a 1-inch border around edge of skillet. (Cake needs room to expand.)

Bake cake until golden brown and firm to the touch, about 25 to 30 minutes. Remove cake from oven and cool in skillet on a wire rack for 3 minutes, then invert onto a platter. Serve warm with crème fraîche or sour cream, if desired.

SERVES 6 TO 8

Bourbon Chocolate Cake

Don't be afraid to take a little nip every now and then.

For Cake

2 cups all-purpose flour

1 teaspoon baking soda

⅛ teaspoon salt

1 ¾ cups hot bourbon (hot but not boiled)

¼ cup hot brewed coffee

5 ounces unsweetened baking chocolate,
  chopped into small pieces

½ cup unsalted butter, cut into small pieces

2 cups granulated sugar

1 teaspoon pure vanilla extract

2 eggs, at room temperature

For Chocolate Ganache

12 ounces semisweet chocolate, chopped into
  small pieces

1 cup heavy cream, scalded

To make Cake

Position rack in middle of oven. Preheat oven to 275 degrees F. Butter and lightly flour two (9-inch) round cake pans.

Sift together flour, baking soda, and salt.

In a large bowl, combine bourbon, coffee, chocolate, and butter. Cover tightly with plastic wrap and let stand until chocolate and butter are completely melted, then stir together with a wire whisk. Stir in sugar and allow the mixture to cool completely.

Using the wire whisk, add the flour mixture in two batches, stirring well after each addition. Add vanilla extract and eggs, one at a time, stirring well after each addition.

Pour batter into prepared cake pans. Bake about 35 to 45 minutes, or until cakes bounce back after gentle pressure and a cake tester or toothpick inserted in the center of the cake comes out clean.

Cool the cakes in the pan completely on wire racks. Run a knife around the inside edge of the pan; invert the pan onto a cardboard cake circle or a flat plate. Frost tops of both layers with Chocolate Ganache, stack one of top of the other, and then frost edges.

To make Chocolate Ganache

Place the chocolate in a large metal or heatproof glass bowl. In a medium saucepan, heat cream over medium heat—do not boil.

Pour the scalded cream over the chocolate. Stir to submerge all of the chocolate. Cover the bowl tightly with plastic wrap and let stand until all of the chocolate is melted, about 10 to 15 minutes. Stir the mixture until smooth and shiny, and then cool to room temperature, about 10 to 15 minutes. With a hand mixer on medium speed, beat the room temperature ganache until thick and fluffy.

SERVES 12

Dewberry's Hummingbird Cake

Steeped in southern tradition.

For Cake

3 cups all-purpose flour

2 cups granulated sugar

½ teaspoon salt

2 teaspoons baking soda

1 teaspoon ground cinnamon

3 large eggs, well beaten

1 ¼ cups canola oil

1 ½ teaspoons pure vanilla extract

1 (8-ounce) can crushed pineapple, drained

¾ cup chopped pecans

¼ cup chopped black walnuts

2 cups chopped ripe banana

For Sweet Cream Cheese Icing

2 (8-ounce) packages cream cheese, softened

1 cup butter, softened

2 (16-ounce) boxes confectioners' sugar

2 teaspoons pure vanilla extract

1 cup chopped toasted pecans

To make Cake

Position rack in middle of oven. Preheat oven to 350 degrees F. Grease and lightly flour three 9-inch round cake pans.

In a medium bowl, sift together flour, sugar, salt, baking soda, and cinnamon twice. Add eggs, canola oil, and vanilla. Stir by hand just until dry ingredients are moistened. Do not over mix. Stir in pineapple and nuts. Add bananas and stir just until incorporated.

Divide batter evenly among the three cake pans. Bake for 25 to 30 minutes, or until a toothpick or cake tester inserted in the center of cake comes out clean. Cool in pan on wire rack for 10 minutes; then remove cake from pan and cool completely on a wire rack.

To make Sweet Cream Cheese Icing

In a medium bowl using an electric mixer on medium speed, combine cream cheese and butter, and cream together until smooth. Add confectioners' sugar and continue beating on medium speed until light and fluffy. Stir in vanilla. Frost the tops of all three cake layers, stack atop each other, and then frost edges. Sprinkle pecans over top.

SERVES 12 TO 16

Strawberry Shortcake Biscuits with Sweet Cream

This buttermilk shortcake biscuit uses a food processor to make a quick and easy biscuit. Do not be fooled into thinking this is just for dessert!

For Sweet Cream

1 cup heavy whipping cream

2 tablespoons confectioners' sugar

½ teaspoon vanilla extract

For Filling

¼ cup honey

2 pints fresh, ripe strawberries, hulled
and sliced lengthwise

For Buttermilk Shortcake Biscuits

2 cups all-purpose flour

2 tablespoons double-acting baking powder

1 teaspoon kosher salt

¼ cup granulated sugar

½ cup unsalted butter, chilled and cut into
½-inch pieces

2 large eggs

½ cup buttermilk

4 mint leaves, finely chopped

To make Sweet Cream

In a small mixing bowl, beat whipping cream, confectioners' sugar, and vanilla until small peaks form; set aside.

To make Filling

In a medium bowl, drizzle honey over the strawberries; set aside.

To make Buttermilk Shortcake Biscuits

Preheat oven to 400 degrees F. Line a large sheet pan with parchment paper.

In a food processor, pulse together flour, baking powder, salt, and sugar. Add butter and pulse to a coarse meal.

In a separate small bowl, mix together eggs and buttermilk. Add egg mixture to the flour mixture in the food processor, and pulse just until the dough comes together. Dough should be sticky. Turn dough onto a lightly floured surface and knead three or four times. Roll the dough to a thickness of 1 inch. Using a 3-inch biscuit cutter lightly dipped in flour, cut out 8 biscuits. Arrange biscuits on prepared sheet pan, leaving about ¼ inch between them. Bake for 20 to 25 minutes. Split biscuits in half. Divide bottom halves among eight plates. Layer with the macerated strawberries and a small pinch of mint. Cover each with a biscuit top and a big dollop of Sweet Cream.

SERVES 8

HAPPY ENDINGS

Caramelized Sweet Grits

People scream for sweet seconds.

2 cups water
2 cups light cream or half-and-half
Pinch of salt
1 ¼ cups quick grits

1 teaspoon vanilla
½ cup unsalted butter
¾ cup sugar
Brown sugar, to caramelize

In a deep pot, bring water, cream, and salt to a boil. Using a whisk, pour grits in a steady stream into the liquid. Continue to whisk on medium-high heat until grits thicken. Reduce to medium heat and continue to stir until grits are thick but not pasty. Turn heat off. Add vanilla, butter, and sugar and mix well. Pour cooked grits into a 9 x 9-inch baking dish and allow to cool and set. You may place in the refrigerator to use the next day. Grits should be firm before caramelizing.

To caramelize grits, sprinkle top with enough brown sugar to cover in a thin layer. Place under broiler until sugar bubbles and melts. You may need to turn pan for even browning. Watch closely, and be careful not to burn the sugar, or yourself!

MAKES 6 SERVINGS

Blueberry Buckle

We serve this for breakfast at the cafe, but I serve buckle for dessert at home.

For Buckle

2 cups all-purpose flour

2 teaspoons baking powder

¾ teaspoon salt

4 tablespoons butter

¾ cup sugar

1 egg

½ cup milk

2 teaspoons grated lemon zest

1 teaspoon lemon juice

2 cups fresh blueberries

For Crumble

⅓ cup sugar

¼ cup flour

1 teaspoon cinnamon

2 tablespoons butter

To make Buckle

Sift flour, baking powder and salt into a medium mixing bowl. In another medium mixing bowl, cream the butter and sugar together. Add the egg to butter mixture and whip until light and fluffy. Add flour mixture, milk, lemon zest, and juice to the creamed mixture. Use your hands to gently fold in blueberries. Place in greased 9 x 9-inch baking pan.

To make Crumble

In a bowl, mix sugar, flour, and cinnamon together. Cut in butter until crumbly. Sprinkle over batter. Bake at 375 degrees F for 45 minutes.

Notes

Metric Conversion Chart

Liquid and Dry Measures

U.S.	Canadian	Australian
$1/4$ teaspoon	1 mL	1 ml
$1/2$ teaspoon	2 mL	2 ml
1 teaspoon	5 mL	5 ml
1 Tablespoon	15 mL	20 ml
$1/4$ cup	50 mL	60 ml
$1/3$ cup	75 mL	80 ml
$1/2$ cup	125 mL	125 ml
$2/3$ cup	150 mL	170 ml
$3/4$ cup	175 mL	190 ml
1 cup	250 mL	250 ml
1 quart	1 liter	1 litre

Temperature Conversion Chart

Fahrenheit	Celsius
250	120
275	140
300	150
325	160
350	180
375	190
400	200
425	220
450	230
475	240
500	260

Index